MW01135816

words matter series

HOW TO WRITE A BOOK

10 SIMPLE STEPS:
THINK LIKE A READER &
WRITE LIKE A BESTSELLING AUTHOR

JULEE BRAND

ONBrand **BOOKS**

an imprint of W. Brand Publishing

Nashville, Tennessee

Author has no responsibility for the persistence or accuracy of URLs for external or third-party Internet Websites referred to in this publication and does not guarantee that any content on such websites is, or will remain, accurate or appropriate.

Information in this book is based on the real-world publishing industry experience of the author at the time of publishing. Changes in the industry may render some information obsolete.

ONBrand Books is an imprint of W. Brand Publishing

For information contact: j.brand@wbrandpub.com

Cover design: designchik.net

How to Write a Book /JuLee Brand—1st ed.

Paperback ISBN: 978-1-956906-71-4

eBook ISBN: 978-1-956906-72-1

CONTENTS

"We tell ourselves stories in order to live."
–Joan Didion

FOREWORD

When I started writing this book, I thought my direction was clear and focused; I would instruct writers how to write a book that spoke to their readers. However, as I gathered research and studied the secrets of best-selling authors, I became increasingly disconnected from my goal, not because of my findings, but because of my approach. My voice became clinical and disingenuous. Though my initial intention remains the same, my voice shifted from teacher to student.

This book shows you a behind the curtain view of writing a book, how to focus, plan, and critique your writing based on your target reader. It will not instruct how to tell a story, which would cover topics like character development, story pacing and arc, and world building, but it will lay the foundation and prepare you to write a book that speaks to your reader.

I sit in the dark, staring at the soft glow of my laptop, hoping my muse likes my new direction. The first paragraph can be the hardest . . . or the easiest; I'll let you decide.

INTRODUCTION

As an aspiring author, you have a burning desire to share your story with others. You have a concept, maybe even the first few pages written, but then your focus derails, you wander down rabbit holes, and question why you ever thought you could do this. This is a common problem for newbies and seasoned writers alike. Through planning and focus, you will jump this hurdle and begin writing a book that connects directly to your readers.

This book is the next step; you've taken the first step to bring your desire into fruition. Learning tried-and-true techniques which can apply to all genres and writing levels will help you finish your first book and be useful as long as you continue writing.

Writing is challenging. Even best-selling writers will say this. I'm not talking about the technicalities of writing like sentence structure and spelling; I'm referring to the organization of thoughts and conveying them so readers will enjoy. An editor will help with the technicalities if you have trouble in that area. Proofreaders also will catch your mistakes; and if you think talented writers don't make mistakes, you probably have read nothing on the Top 10 lists lately.

Every writer is unique, just as every person is unique. Some need a set schedule, while others can only write when the muse hits them. There are those who need total silence, while others must have music playing. Some write about one subject only and while others write in many genres. There are a thousand differences between one writer and the next; but they all have one thing in common: the desire to express themselves through the written word.

As I lay out techniques, each like threads to weave throughout your story, you will see how your characters and plots intertwine into the hearts and minds of your readers. You'll answer these questions and more: Why does your story need to be told? Who is it for? How will it unfold? Are you ready to carve out your own slice of literary legacy?

So, who am *I*? I am JuLee Brand, an award-winning independent hybrid boutique publisher and aspiring author. As a publisher, I guide authors through writing and publishing processes to bring their stories to life. But as an author, I struggle with every step in this book. I write this to help you avoid frustration and enjoy the writer's journey to publishing your best book. You will find the culmination of my experience throughout these pages: a roadmap to writing a book that weaves the needs of your readers with the soul of your narrative, ensuring your words are not only read but connect.

I believe everyone has a story and this passion for the story led me to create my publishing company; W. Brand Publishing, where I help writers transform their experiences into memoirs that inspire the reader and fiction books that entertain and captivate. There is nothing so satisfying to me than seeing an author receive their first published book and achieving their dream.

Writers submit many stories to my company; some are great, but others, well, those are the ones we didn't publish. The outstanding books all had one thing in common; they kept me turning the pages. It didn't matter if the books were fiction or nonfiction; they held my interest as a reader.

Throughout this book, I'll share the key steps that writers use to connect to readers and real-life examples that will help make those steps achievable. Also, included:

- Simple 10-step process to write a book–One Step per chapter
- Determining and achieving your goals for the book
- How to create your perfect target reader
- Build a plan for your book that makes it hard NOT to finish
- Writing assignments to put into practice the chapter highlights
- Overview of publishing models–Pros and Cons

Upon completion of this book, you will have not only ten proven techniques in your writing toolbox, but a master template to use for any genre you choose to write, a guide to the best-sellers that live in your mind. This is not just about writing; it's the art of transforming thoughts into creative communication.

These steps are more than mere suggestions; they are philosophies which create a deep connection to the reader with every word. From tapping into the profound reasons that drive you to write to intimately knowing your reader, and from the meticulous development of your book's concept and characters to the triumphant moment of publication, each step takes you closer to the end of each writing journey.

OK, you're probably wondering, "Can it really be that straightforward?" Doubt is a natural companion to creation, echoing in your head that the reality between an idea and a finished book is but a fool's dream. However, doubt is also the first obstacle we conquer together. You will find clarity in intention, precision in planning, and the fortitude to forge your narrative with unwavering confidence as we finish each step.

Close your eyes for a moment and imagine holding your finished book, flipping through its pages filled with words you wrote–the words that came from your mind and soul; its eye-catching cover and the feel of the paper's texture, each chapter a testament to achieving your dream. Feel the weight of this accomplishment; hear the echo of your message reaching into the hearts of readers. This vision is closer to reality now. You will write not just any book, but one that resonates with your readers, one that aligns with the compelling narratives of best-selling authors.

Writing a book is a commitment, not just to the craft of writing, but to the profound impact your words will have. You are not merely stringing sentences together; you are crafting experiences, shaping thoughts, and creating human connection.

Let's start at the beginning, where every great story does—with understanding your *why*. The goal lies not only in the destination but in understanding and enjoying the journey. You are standing at the edge of an unknown territory full of promise. You've made your choice to write; your adventure has already begun.

The act of writing is not a sprint but a marathon, promising more than just accomplishment—it promises transformation.

Grab your writing tool of choice. Deep breath. You've got this.

START WITH WHY

"Our passion lies deep in who we are, not what we do."–Simon Sinek

This quote by Simon Sinek in his book *Start with Why* stresses that our passion, at our core, is who we are as humans, not our occupation or actions. As writers, we must think about that as we craft our stories so that our message is genuine and resonates with our readers.

Writing a book that is significant, influential, and gratifying requires having a firm grasp of your "why."

FINDING YOUR *WHY*

Your *why* is the underlying motivation that leads you to write a book. Your *why* is the driving force that keeps you going when you lose focus; it's the answer to, "Why do I want to write this book?" and "Who am I?" It is your touchstone incentive to keep going.

Simon Sinek conveyed the importance of finding your why in his book *Start with Why*, "When we know WHY we do what we do, everything falls into place. When we don't, we have to push things into place." Even when writing is difficult, frustrating, or when you are going through writer's block, your why pushes you to start again and finish. There are readers depending on it, but more on that later. Your why makes sure the message of the book is genuine and not contrived.

Visualizing the desired outcome of your writing serves as the next step. What emotions course through your body when envisioning yourself as a published author? Joy? Pride? Relief? Use this vivid imagery to fuel your motivation visualization. Detail the impact you foresee your book having—on yourself and your readers—and let this vision guide your commitment.

Dive in, ask the hard questions and be brutally honest with yourself; self-deception serves no one in this process. Be vulnerable, allowing your core motivation to be revealed. Exploration is key in discovering your motivation, your vision, and your audience; revisiting this when the journey gets tough is a reminder of why you started and why you must continue.

To be successful in this exercise, your why should resonate with you on a profound level. It should feel like a truth that has always been a part of you, now given a voice through your words.

I'll use myself as an example. My why, my core belief that gets me out of bed every day, is I am making the world a better place by creating platforms to create greater human connection; I truly believe that everyone's story should be told to empower a world with kindness and empathy. Yeah, I go big or go home, but seriously, even though my why may seem lofty to some, it is what drives me to my core and makes me enjoy what I do and keeps me focused.

If you struggle to pinpoint your why, seek inspiration from others. Sinek's book, *Start with Why* will help you understand the why concept on a larger and personal scale, but reading author interviews, exploring biographies, and engaging with the writing community will help you find the why for your story. Sometimes, the spark *you* need comes from the stories of others.

UNDERSTANDING THE *WHY* OF YOUR STORY

Every journey begins with one step and in the journey to write a book, that step is determining *why* you're writing at all.

Maybe you are writing to inspire others by sharing your knowledge and expertise, or perhaps simply to tell a compelling story. Whatever your motivation, understanding your why will keep you focused and committed to your writing goals. "People don't buy what you do; they buy why you do it. And what you do simply proves what you believe," Sinek states in *Start with Why*. In this case, what you do is conveyed through your story.

Perhaps your story why is to write a best-selling book. Many aspiring authors hope their book captivates readers enough to land on a best-seller list. But as wonderful as that accolade seems, many authors soon feel like they're missing something even when they reach that goal. What is the secret recipe which authors follow when setting personal goals? It all comes back to why.

If the only why for your story is to achieve accolades, your books may lack connection to the reader. Stories written with the readers' needs as the why, are the books that not only receive accolades but produce long-term fans and happier authors.

To demonstrate this theory, I'll use a couple of examples that should drive home the message. For decades, advertisers touted the superiority of their products and told YOU why you should buy them, but alas, consumers grew wise to this vernacular. As we watched more competition among products flood the market, we grew skeptical of their motivations; surely not every product could be the best.

Because of this skepticism, startups began sharing the heart of why they do what they do, why their products or services matter. Many companies now highlight how giving back and providing safe and inviting workplaces is their priority. It is the honesty and transparency of the communication that endears the consumer to a company and therefore, their products.

Can you see how this relates to writing books? First, putting in writing the why for the book helps us define what we are trying to accomplish–our message. Some detail is useful here, as merely having a desire to "write a best-selling fiction book" doesn't give much direction. However, stating well-defined whys for writing the book such as, "I want to write a book that shows how to manage PTSD through the following forms of therapy" or "My survival journey through combat and how I manage PTSD" create a direct bond with your target reader.

Knowing your why ensures your book will differ from other books on the market. You might think there's no need for another book about needlepoint, intergalactic space travel, or air conditioning repair, but that's merely a sign that you're undervaluing your vision. There are always people who need a new perspective, and you might have the one the reader connects with.

It doesn't matter what you are writing or how motivated you are to complete it; you will struggle to get through to the end if you do not know your why. Focus on the message you want readers to take away when they have read every word and closed the book. What will they remember?

A good way to make sure you don't lose focus on the why is to leave yourself a note—on the wall, above your desk, on your computer monitor—wherever you can see it while you write. This note is a constant reminder to keep you on track with your goal and why you're writing this book. Each book you write will have its own why, just as you have your own why for becoming an author.

My personal story why is to help writers set themselves up to achieve their own successful book by showing how focus and preparation can lay the groundwork for a story that resonates with their readers.

HERE ARE FOUR PROMPTS TO ASSIST YOU IN DEFINING YOUR STORY *WHY*:

What are you passionate about? What lights you up? What topics could you talk about freely for hours with no prep time?

This could be as simple as writing about your love for Lhasa-poos or as complex as your insight into indoor herb gardening for sustainability. It is that passion for a topic that will keep your interest and your reader will connect with the vibrancy of your words.

Still having a hard time narrowing down a topic? Think about your interests: sports you play, your hobbies, favorite TV shows, movies, who you follow on TikTok; these interests could lead you to write a unique or improved narrative than what is currently in print. Toni Morrison has a great quote, "If there's a book that you want to read, but it hasn't been written yet, then you must write it." Treat this quote as a quest, a challenge.

The key to a unique story is your original take on it. This stems from excitement about your why and your words, which combined, create a new take on a topic written about many times.

The standout books submitted to my publishing company, whether a memoir with an underlying mental health theme or an espionage thriller, all have new slants on the message. Your books need that too. Make your book stand out from the crowd—be creative. With a unique idea and a bit of hard work, the only limitations are those you put on yourself—the only limit is your imagination!

What is your message? What is the takeaway of the book? What will your reader learn or feel?

If you are writing a nonfiction book, become the expert in your field when sharing your experience. Being able to share knowledge and teach readers how to overcome problems or learn a new skill can be an excellent why.

Fiction stories also need to have an obvious message. Is it a good vs. evil theme? Perhaps the narrative is to teach kindness through improbable characters. Whatever your theme, your story why must be the takeaway of the book.

Who is your audience?

People buy books because they want to get something out of them. With fiction, they want to be entertained, escaping from their ordinary lives. With nonfiction, they may want help in learning something new, or perhaps they want to feel they aren't alone. In either case, people buy books expecting the investment of time and money will fill a need or want in their life.

You will factor your reader in after determining *your* personal why. What are the wants, needs, and preferences of the demographics of your key audience? What type of influence do you hope to have on their lives? How can you ease their pain points? What can you offer them that someone else can't?

Knowing your target audience will enable you to write a book suited to their wants, preferences, and interests and ensure that your message is well-received. We'll explore how to find and define your target reader in Step 2.

How will you define success?

Obviously, you want your book to be a success, but what does that mean to you? Nearly everyone defines success differently; using someone else's definition may not be what rings true for you.

Our society often measures success only financially. While that can be an obvious and useful measurement of success; it might not be the benchmark you set. Many writers make a nice living as career authors and, for others, the financial gain is not as important as knowing their stories connected with readers and changed lives.

If monetary gain is as important to you as changing lives, please consider it may take time to build an audience of faithful readers; it can literally take years. Many new writers with dreams only of financial success become disheartened when royalties don't add up as quickly or fully as expected.

Publishing is patience. Dream big but be in it for the long game. Perhaps your first book flops, but your second reignites sales of the first or maybe you write a series that doesn't get noticed until book three or after you write a completely different genre. If your dream and your *why* is to be an author, time is relative, just ask Albert Einstein.

It is because of this time relativity which makes defining your success so important in the early planning process. I will emphasize again that if your definition is only financial, this could be a long journey, however, if you set small attainable goals like winning awards or becoming an Amazon best seller in your category as well as larger goals, you will celebrate more victories along the way. Part of enjoying the journey of writing is celebrating hitting milestones.

STEP 1 WRITING EXERCISE

In this chapter, we've talked about finding your why and how it plays an essential part in writing any book. The why must come from deep within *you*; it's not something that someone else can do for you. Many times, finding your why can be the hardest part, but it is so essential. Do not skip this step.

For this exercise, answer the five prompts to help define your why for writing the book, your message, who is your audience, what genre will you write, and how will you define a successful book.

- What are you passionate about?
- What is your message?
- What genre will you write in?
- How do you define your success?
- Who is your audience?

KNOW YOUR READER

"I can't write without a reader. It's precisely like a kiss—you can't do it alone."–John Cheever

It is very important to know who your audience is before you start writing. What are their needs and interests, and what do they hope to gain from reading your work?

However, new writers often write to a "generic" reader, without truly understanding who that reader is. Their error is in focusing on the message *they* want to convey, rather than how the *reader* will receive the message or if they want it at all.

Perhaps the hardest genre for first-time authors to write is biography or memoir. While you may think, *It's MY story, I'll write it MY way,* but shelves are full and online carts are empty because *MY* way didn't speak to the reader. This "my way" approach usually stems from friends and family telling you incessantly how you must write a book. While I agree with the sentiment that everyone has a story, unless you are writing only to leave your legacy, you will need to think about who, aside from people you know, will want to read your book. Authors writing "my way" many times will alienate an audience who may have benefited from their experiences instead of helping a reader through their own pain and struggles if written with them specifically in mind.

Of course, when first asked, writers will say they want EVERYONE to read their book, but trying to write for all those different people at the same time is literally impossible. From one point of view, that makes sense, since we want as wide a readership for our books as possible. There's just one thing . . . not everyone is the same. We all have different likes, interests, and ways of expressing ourselves. We have different beliefs, different political positions, even different ball teams we cheer for. Trying to write for everyone at the same time is literally impossible. You'd have to write so broadly it would appear shallow, and no one will connect with it at all.

Writing is one of the most personal forms of communication there is. When we speak, words often leave our lips without thinking; thoughts may be incomplete and easily misunderstood. But when mis-communicated words arise in the writing process, we stop to think about what we've written, reword it, sometimes multiple times, until it comes out right. Our message is clear and concise because we have the luxury of time and editing.

The good news is that you have an ideal reader out there, even though you may not know who they are yet. That ideal reader will be someone who wants what you have to share. They have a specific life and specific personality, and you need to be writing to them, just as if you were writing a letter. You don't write a love letter the same way in which you write a business letter, and you wouldn't write that business letter like a letter to your mother. Granted, letter writing is fast becoming a thing of the past; but the idea still holds. We write letters to a particular person, expressing ourselves to them specifically. Nobody writes a letter without a pretty good idea who they were writing it to and what the person was like.

Yet new writers often write to a "generic" reader, without truly understanding who that reader is. They lose track of who we are writing for. This leads to a disconnect of the message they want to convey versus who they want to convey that message to. In doing so, they end up with a book that doesn't have an audience.

This is especially true of authors who write memoirs. They want to share their life experiences. So, they write it without thinking about who they are writing it for, who will read it. The result is a narrative that many times reads like a very long informative article or a self-serving replay of their life. Poorly focused memoirs miss the mark and therefore neglect the opportunity to help or teach readers through the writer's life experiences. With a vision of their target reader, the story helps the reader through their personal pain and struggles.

Knowing who you are writing for will affect everything you do in creating your book. For starters, it will affect the language you use to communicate with them. Different communities of people use different terminology to express things. If you're writing to a particular group of people, you want to use the terminology that they use. Different ages, industries, and genres also have guidelines to stay within.

Before you put the first word on paper, you've got to know who it is that you're writing for. So, how do you find that person?

Here's the secret…you don't. You make them up instead.

In the world of marketing, they create an avatar of their ideal customer. This avatar is the person they are developing their products and advertising for. Research will go into as much detail about that person as possible, defining everything from their clothing style to their favorite television show: concerns and pains, joys and sorrows. People who are part of that marketing team will know that avatar as well as they know their own mothers and talk about that avatar as if it was a real person. They'll even name them.

I know, you're saying "OK, so how do I create my ideal reader avatar and superfan?"

Creating your ideal reader/superfan starts in your imagination. Imagine yourself as the fan of your work. Start analyzing what the fan would expect from you as a writer, what things the book should talk about and what the overall feel/tone of the book should be like. This person adores your writing and is a perfect example of your intended demographic.

Creating an image of your superfan/ideal reader and thinking from their perspective will help you write a book that appeals to them. This reader profile will be useful for all genres.

There's a good chance that you already have some idea in mind of who you're writing for.

Here are some questions to help visualize your perfect reader image:

- How old are they?
- Where do they live geographically? Do they rent or own their home? Do they live with their parents or relatives?
- What is their ethnicity?
- What is their gender? What are their pronouns? Are they part of the LGBTQIA+ community?
- Do they have hobbies or interests? Avid skier? Aspiring homebrew master? Novice welder?

- Where do they shop? Are they fashionable or ambivalent to trends? Walmart or Target?
- What motivates them? Politics? Music? Dance? Success?
- What are their personal values? Are they religious? Do they want to change the world?
- What are their daily pain points and concerns?
- What is their relationship status? Single? Married? Dating?
- Do they have kids or are they a kid?
- What kinds of food do they eat? What restaurants do they go to?

These are not the only questions you can ask, but it will give you a good place to start when crafting your perfect reader. When you understand your audience in depth, you will connect to readers and build your superfans. Digging deeper into the profile of who your reader is will enable you to write to them like you've known them your entire life.

Don't expect to finish this in an afternoon. You might come up with the basic avatar quickly, but you'll need to do some research too, filling out details about their personality, interests, and especially their pain points. This research is critical if you are going to write a book that connects to them.

HOW YOUR AUDIENCE HELPS DEFINE THE STORY

Knowing who you are writing to affects many aspects in creating your book, including:

LANGUAGE AND TERMINOLOGY

By knowing your audience, you will write in vernacular they understand. For example, if you are writing a self-help book, you will want to use language that speaks to the audience by emphasizing the pain point they want to solve in language that is straightforward and casual. While you may need some technical terms, follow these with simple explanations so your reader grasps the concepts if the terms are not common.

GENRE

It is also very important to consider what readers expect from the genre you've chosen to write in. Even when writing an original story, you must pay attention to the genre; fantasy and thrillers have two unique styles of writing just as romance and business books do.

While genre blending is common, again, make sure the story's narrative follows what the readers want. A very popular trend in self-help is to add personal stories, creating a blending of self-help and memoir genres, with the primary focus being to help readers; or perhaps it's the other way around, a memoir with advice learned through the writer's life journey. Fiction genre blending is very common with Sci-Fi romance or just about any other genre mixed with romance.

Research the top writers in the genre you choose and pay attention to story tropes (common themes, plot structures and devices, and/or storylines). Examples of tropes are good vs. evil, rich girl falls for the bad boy, and businessperson shares the story of transformation from homeless child to building a successful brand then gives back to the community.

AGE

Knowing the age group of your perfect reader is very important. There is leeway here, as many in their 20s and well into their 90s enjoy young adult fiction. However, don't put yourself in the "writing for everyone" conundrum. Having your perfect reader in mind will help narrow the age range.

NEED

For your book to succeed, it must meet a need in your reader's life. That need may be for nothing more than entertainment; but don't take that lightly. Entertaining people can be one of the most challenging needs to meet, as it is quite subjective. It's imperative to have a clear focus on who the intended audience is and their preferences.

Your reader chooses your book because they connect on some level to the problem you will solve. Usually, that connection happens only by reading the back cover copy, so it is important that this, too, connects concisely to your target audience.

COMPARATIVE TITLE RESEARCH (KNOWN AS COMP TITLES)

Consider what other books in your genre have to say about the subject. You can use this to find market gaps and a chance to set yourself apart from the competition. Consider which subjects are trending and what topics are lacking.

One easy way is to read what others have written, specifically focusing on books that have been successful and widely accepted by readers. This is a good place to start, but always keep your ideal reader in mind when researching the titles. Even if your topic may be the same, comp titles may vary by intended audience.

By analyzing and understanding comp titles, an author can craft a book that resonates deeply with readers, increasing the likelihood of its commercial success. This claim is based on concrete evidence, best-seller lists, reader reviews, and industry analytics.

STEP 2 WRITING ASSIGNMENT

Visualize, in detail, your ideal reader
Use all your research and brainstorming. What is the person's age, gender, profession, interests, and any other pertinent details? Examine their inclinations, principles, and outlooks. Look past the obvious details and discover their real wants and desires. What do they look like?

Detail their struggles and pain points
Consider the difficulties, issues, or pain points that your target reader might deal with. What challenges do they face in their own lives or in the area that your work deals with? Answering these questions will better adapt your book's content to offer solutions, insights, or inspiration when you are aware of their challenges.

Describe the results the reader seeks.
Think about the goals your ideal reader would like to achieve. What are their objectives, dreams, or aspirations? How can your book assist people in overcoming obstacles, gaining knowledge, or enhancing their lives? Is it only to entertain? An understanding of this information will guide writing about what your readers are looking for, ensuring its relevance and worth.

How will your reader feel after completing your book?
Will they feel hopeful? Will they be anxious about your
next book? Are they more knowledgeable on a topic?
They should feel exactly what you intended from your
story why.

STEP 3

DEVELOP YOUR CHARACTERS

"First, find out what your hero wants, then just follow him."—Ray Bradbury

B radbury knew the secret to writing a fascinating story is to concentrate on the protagonist's aspirations, objectives, and goals and let them direct the story. To write a novel that is interesting, emotionally resonant, and fulfilling for the reader, the writer must follow the hero's path and the challenges they encounter in achieving their objectives.

Knowing your reader is also critical as you develop your book's characters. One of the most essential parts of character development is ensuring that your reader can identify with them. In fiction, you want readers to live vicariously through the character's experiences, making the character so relatable that they leap into the character's life. In nonfiction, it's imperative that the reader connect to the author, the problem they are solving, or the situation they lived through.

DYNAMIC CHARACTERS

Whether fiction or nonfiction, character development is important. This entails giving each character a distinctive personality, backstory, and motive that guides their actions and choices throughout the plot. Creating a character arc, which is how the character evolves and changes over the story, is a common starting point; it is a crucial component enabling connection with the characters more profoundly and developing emotional attachments to their difficulties, accomplishments, and shortfalls. Writers can explore significant themes, relay information, and increase the relatability and impact of their stories by using well thought-out characters.

Character growth is essential to enable readers to relate to the storyline and the concepts it presents; it draws in readers and keeps them interested in the story. Authors who plan their character development create fiction or nonfiction that is more enjoyable and memorable to the readers.

A range of strategies, including backstory formation, conflicts both internal and external, connections and interactions, and the power of decision-making, helps construct characters. A realistic character should have complicated motives, ambitions, and imperfections, as well as distinct strengths and weaknesses.

Nonfiction, such as a memoir, relies on the reader's connection to the characters and storyline arc just like fiction. Characters in nonfiction highlight points, strengthen claims, and give the reader a relevant viewpoint. A good memoir or biography has a conflict the author overcomes personally. They will have relationships with others, many of whom easily fit into typical character types.

In business or self-help books, authors are also the main character. Their expertise is important in making difficult ideas and concepts more approachable and interesting. This encourages readers to engage with the content more deeply. Even though nonfiction works frequently address abstract or complex topics, authors should give specific instances and real-world examples to explain experiences and commentary to establish a connection with the reader. Remember to incorporate real-life stories full of personality, internal monologue to reveal hidden depth, and personal stories about your experience in the field you are writing about. Those stories can be about mistakes you've made, victories you've had, or challenges you've overcome.

Side note: It is important to get permission if you wish to use the real names of the characters in your biography, memoir, or any nonfiction book aside from citing quotations. If you don't feel comfortable asking for permission, consider three things: 1) changing their name, gender, or location to alleviate any confusion with a real person, 2) reconsider their portion of the story, or 3) consult a lawyer familiar with defamation.

CRAFTING PERFECT AND IMPERFECT CHARACTERS

The art of crafting characters depends on the lens through which the writer allows them to be seen. But it is only from the reader's view that the characters come to life; ignoring this perspective causes the story to fall flat.

FIVE COMPONENTS USED IN BOTH FICTION AND NON-FICTION WRITING

Understand Character Roles in Story Tropes

Creating characters that leap off the page and capture the hearts of readers is an art form. As you embark on this journey, your objective is to breathe life into your protagonists, antagonists, and the supporting cast, making them as real as the people you encounter daily.

Study books in your genre to observe nonfiction and fiction characters.

Research and Relatable Characters
Gather your tools: a character profile template (or a simple notebook), access to psychological resources or character studies for reference, and an open heart to empathize with your fictional creations. Also, observe the world around you; people-watching can be one of the greatest sources of inspiration.

Character Motivations and Actions
Consider the keywords that lay the groundwork for the discussion of character motivation: empathy, relatability, audience, experience, and perception. These terms serve as the bridge between writer and reader in order to resonate with the reader.

Digging into what drives each character, their desires and motivation, adds a deeper understanding to their relationships and actions in the story.

Personality
Directly related to character motivation is their personality and voice. Once you have determined what makes the character tick, you will have a closer understanding of the character's voice and characteristics, how they respond to others, their dialogue, and consequent actions.

Are they grumpy or content, optimistic or pessimistic? How does their personality blend with the rest of the characters in the story, or does it repel? Are they the antagonist or protagonist?

Transformation and Growth
It's critical to depict the character's development and evolution throughout the story. This entails illustrating the character's struggles and setbacks, as well as how they overcame them to develop into a transformed person. The ideas and concepts being conveyed in the story must have a plausible impact on the character's development and change. The transformation must be realistic about how the character would respond to these challenges in life.

STEP 3 WRITING EXERCISE

Character development is frequently associated with fiction writing, but it is just as crucial to give your nonfiction work life by developing interesting, sympathetic characters. You will find much similarity between character creation and creating your ideal reader.

Here is a brief writing assignment to help you identify your story's main characters:

1. **Identify the main individuals in your book:** Make a list of the key characters who will appear frequently in your fiction/nonfiction writing. These could be authorities, real-world examples, historical people, or completely fictional amalgamations. Consider only those who best represent the primary concepts or themes of your work.
2. **Describe their experiences and backgrounds:** Investigate the pasts of one or two of the main

characters on your list; recount their personal backgrounds, mentioning any pertinent events, accomplishments, or education.

3. **Create scenarios that motivate each of the characters and how they will interact with each other:** Go deep into the personality profiles of each character.

4. What events create the transformation or growth of the characters?

5. What message do you want readers to take away from the story?

DEFINE YOUR STORY

"We are all storytellers. We all live in a network of stories. There isn't a stronger connection between people than storytelling."–Jimmy Neil Smith, Director of the International Storytelling Center

As Jimmy Neil Smith says, people live in a network of stories and there is no stronger thing that connects us all than storytelling. This quote should give hope to all who have imposter syndrome about writing just because they hear a voice in their head saying, "I'm not a writer." No matter your skill level of writing, what matters most is the story and, as Mr. Smith says, "We are all storytellers."

Defining your story is not just describing scene after scene, the writer must immerse the reader into the story using language that captivates all the senses. Words matter and it's key that the author creates a reality that absorbs the reader. As you read through the structure of a story, visualize how these pertain to your story, nonfiction or fiction.

Let's dissect these components one by one, fleshing out their intricacies. The setup introduces your characters and their world, grounding your reader in the calm and normality before the storm. It is here where you will plant the seeds of your protagonist's desires and the impending conflict. What is their world like? What is about to change? This is the foundation upon which everything else will stand.

Intrigue sharpens when the inciting incident crashes into the narrative. This moment catapults your protagonist into a whirlwind of change, challenging their desires and setting them on a path of confrontation. How does this event shift the status quo? Why must your character act?

Rising action builds the tension, as your character faces obstacles that test their resolve. Here, you'll weave subplots and secondary characters into the main thread, enriching the tapestry of your tale. What trials must they endure? How do they grow? Remember, each hurdle should bring them closer to—or further from—their ultimate resolve.

Careful handling of plot twists, the unexpected turns which keep readers on their toes is imperative. They must make sense within the context of your story, even if they shock or surprise. Can you see the hidden paths within your narrative, those that lead to revelations and reversals?

The climax is the pinnacle of your story, the moment of highest tension and drama. Here, your protagonist confronts their greatest challenge. How will they fare when all forces converge against them? The emotional weight of your story hangs in the balance.

Following the climax, the falling action allows both your character and your reader to catch their collective breath. The consequences of the climax unfold, leading toward closure. What did the character learn? What did they lose or gain?

Finally, the ending ties the remaining threads, offering resolution and a glimpse into the new status quo. How has the world changed? How has the character transformed?

Should you encounter stumbling blocks, such as plot holes or lackluster characters, revisit your focus–your why. Sometimes, a fresh perspective or a return to the basics can reinvigorate your writing and clarify your vision.

With this comprehensive overview, it's time to roll up your sleeves and begin the meticulous task of crafting your story's skeleton. As you piece together the bones of your narrative, infuse each scene with vivid imagery, making your world leap off the page. Use direct questions to challenge your characters and, by extension, your readers. Keep your language simple, yet evocative, ensuring the heart of your story is strong.

6 STEPS TO DEFINE YOUR STORY

Takeaway/Theme/Motif

What is the takeaway of the story? What is the motif thread that draws you from the first page to last?

It matters not whether you write fiction or nonfiction; a writer must decide the focus of the book. When the reader finishes the book, what is the principal theme they remember?

Without a theme or thread connecting the story, readers may easily get lost or, worse, become bored with the narrative. Taking the time to define not only your story and characters but *your* why becomes critical when all the pieces are being assembled. Your research's reward staves off writer's block, creating a theme and characters that readers love. Thematic examples in fiction are good prevailing evil and dramatic transformation of characters; nonfiction takeaways could include persuasion of ideas, lifestyle changes, and empathy.

Timeline
Once you have your takeaway theme, sketch out the timeline of your story. Using significant events based on traditional story arcs, plot out the structure of the story. This can be as in-depth as you'd like; it could be as simple as an outline or as complex as you want to make it.

The 5 Ws
If you are familiar with journalistic writing, you know that the 5 Ws are who, what, where, when, and why. Using your prior research in character development and finding your why, figuring out the motivation and actions of each character in relation to the story by answering the 5 Ws should help solidify the timeline.

Conflict Events
Refer to your timeline and pull out the major significant events where there is conflict. Conflict generates tension and drama to keep readers interested; it could be an internal conflict with the protagonist or perhaps an environmental issue. It's critical to recognize the primary conflicts by exploiting them to advance the plot.

This recognition is the same for fiction and nonfiction. Whether the dark side tempts your hero, or a toxic narcissist creates struggles in your life, these pivotal plot points must be thoroughly planned for the story structure.

Plot Twist

Your novel can also advance and keep readers on the edge of their seats with a clever plot surprise. Lock in readers' interest by including a startling scene in the narrative to intrigue them and keep the plot moving. You will see this done many times in thrillers and crime novels.

In nonfiction, an unexpected shocking viewpoint or piece of information that refutes common beliefs could give the story a fresh take and be a welcome addition to the reader.

Story Structure

To write a book that appeals to readers, as mentioned before, you need to be familiar with story structures for the genre you choose to write.

The Three-Act format, which divides the narrative into the setup, confrontation, and resolution, is a popular fiction storytelling format. The setup introduces the protagonist and their environment, and in the confrontation, the protagonist deals with difficulties and roadblocks that lead to a climax. After the climax, the story can end with a resolution.

The Problem-Solution framework is a well-liked story framework for nonfiction authors. With this format, you identify the issue your readers are experiencing before offering a remedy. This is an excellent method to keep readers interested while also giving them useful knowledge to help them live better lives.

The Narrative Form is another strong nonfiction structure. To communicate information and make it more interesting for readers, this includes adopting narrative techniques. Using personal stories and examples from the real world makes your ideas more vivid, accessible, and memorable.

STEP 4 WRITING EXERCISE

Using the previous six steps to define your story, combine this with your Step 3 Writing Exercise regarding your characters.

If you run into any blocks, refer to Step 2 and remember your reader and if that doesn't help, go back to Step 1, your *why*.

You are well on your way now!

STEP 5

CRAFT A WRITING PLAN

"There is nothing harder to estimate than a writer's time, nothing harder to keep track of. There are moments—moments of sustained creation—when his time is fairly valuable; and there are hours and hours when a writer's time isn't worth the paper, he is not writing anything on."–E. B. White

There are a lot of misconceptions about writing a book. Some people have the idea that writing is all about inspiration. To them, writers sit around, wasting their time, until the "inspiration" hits them. Then they turn out page after page of fantastic literature, which will amaze any reader. Birds sing the writer's praises, forest creatures frolic at their feet, and the sun always shines (insert record needle scratch here).

Uh . . . no. Sorry, it doesn't work that way. Inspiration is very important; usually, it's what gets you writing, and probably tied to Step 1, your core why. But once your inspiration muse gifts you the story idea, what do you do now? It won't get the book done for you. Finishing the book comes from discipline and dedication.

Ask any successful writer and they can tell you horror stories about how they've struggled through parts of the story. They didn't get through those difficult sections by waiting till their muse hit them. They pushed through, working out the problem.

Yes, writer's block is real, but serious writers learn tricks to defeat it. When writer's block strikes, writers can jump past the problem area and work on something else to clear their heads then look at the problem passage from a fresh point of view. A large part of their success as a writer comes from their ability to overcome the block, push through, and get the book written.

The key is discipline . . . self-discipline. No one else is going to discipline you; you're going to have to do it yourself. So, before going any further, you need to ask yourself the question, "Am I ready to commit to this book? How can I make a schedule to work on my book consistently?"

Let's talk about that.

In this digital age, cursor and glowing screen replace pen and parchment. A comprehensive writing software is key to make your ideas take shape. Whether it's the standard Microsoft Word or specialized tool like Scrivener, these programs offer more than just a blank canvas; they provide organizational frameworks, formatting options, and sometimes even the ability to track changes and outline your narrative.

ESSENTIAL TOOLS FOR THE SERIOUS WRITER

- **Comprehensive Writing Software:** Microsoft Word, Scrivener, Google Docs
- **Reliable Research Catalog System:** key for organizing folders, documents, links, etc.

- **Inspiring Writing Environment:** a place where your creativity naturally flows
- **Planned Writing Routine:** Set time to write daily or at certain times a week
- **Robust Self-Editing Process**
- **Support Network of Beta Readers and Writing Peers**
- **Professional Editor:** Search Reedsy.com or LinkedIn

Imagine crafting a story with multiple intertwining plots. Writing software and organization structure will help you keep track of each thread, ensuring consistency and coherence in your narrative. The right tool can make timely work of complex stories.

However, stories do not exist in a vacuum. They are the sum of myriad truths and half-truths woven together in the writer's mind. A reliable cataloging system—be it digital folders, cloud storage, or physical files—is the archive of your story's DNA. Apps like Evernote or OneNote can also serve as your external brain, cataloging bits of inspiration.

Consider the historical fiction author who stumbles upon an obscure fact that could become a turning point in their narrative. With an organized research system, this nugget of information is always within reach, ready to be woven into the story at just the right time.

Creativity is often a product of our surroundings. An inspiring writing environment, whether a quiet home office adorned with motivational quotes or a bustling café with robust smells of today's roast, it can make the difference between a fruitful writing session or a barren one. Imagine a space where every element—the light, the sounds, the very air—seems to conspire to help you write. Such a sanctuary can become a sacred site where ideas flow freely, with no distractions.

A consistent routine helps you manage your time, set achievable goals, and make steady progress. Envision the satisfaction of completing your daily writing goal, knowing that each session brings you closer to the finished book. A planned routine turns the daunting task of writing a book into a series of manageable steps.

Commit to a writing schedule that resonates with your lifestyle. Early risers might find their muse in the tranquility of dawn, while night owls may prefer the quiet of evening. Consistency is key; let your chosen time become a sacred ritual, a daily appointment with your imagination that is non-negotiable.

Distractions are the bane of focus. Identify what commonly disrupts your writing flow—be it digital notifications, household chores, or social media—and take proactive measures to minimize these interruptions. Perhaps it's as simple as silencing your phone or as disciplined as a self-imposed internet ban during writing hours.

To ensure these strategies are more than mere aspirations, it's crucial to detail the implementation process. Craft a weekly timetable that allocates specific blocks of time to writing. Use tools, such as digital calendars or planners, to visualize your schedule. Hold yourself accountable by setting reminders or enlisting the support of a writing group or accountability partner who can encourage you to adhere to your plan.

The first draft is just the beginning. A robust self-editing process refines raw thoughts into polished prose but don't self-edit so much you can't progress. After you are comfortable with your story, send to a few beta readers and trusted writer peers who can give you unbiased feedback.

When you feel good about the revised draft from feedback received, seek a professional editor on Reedsy. com or LinkedIn.com. The key to a great story is finding an editor who can take your story to another level, creating a polished product that the reader can't put down.

Remember that the writer's toolkit is not static. It evolves as we do, adapting to your creativity and technology. With these foundational tools at your disposal, you are ready to embark on the noble quest of writing your book, a journey that promises both challenge and reward. And so, with pen—or cursor—poised, let's begin.

SETTING YOUR WRITING GOALS

The aim is simple yet profound: to set writing goals that are not only clear and specific but also inspiring and attainable. The goals you choose will become the backbone of your writing project, the silent motivators that whisper encouragement when the blank page looms, and the muse seems distant.

Gather your materials—a notebook or computer for recording your goals, a calendar for scheduling, and a quiet space for contemplation. Ensure you have a solid grasp on the book you wish to write, including its genre, subject, and the message you hope to convey.

The process of setting writing goals involves reflection, specificity, realistic timeframes, and a touch of audacity. It is a dance of both the practical and the aspirational, a balance between dreaming big and acting with precision and practicality.

As you craft each goal, infuse it with vivid detail. Instead of a nebulous aim like "write more," pledge to "complete 500 words of the first chapter by Wednesday." Assign deadlines that are generous enough to be achievable yet tight enough to instill a sense of urgency.

Beware the burden of perfectionism that may lure you away from progress. Goals should stretch your abilities but not break your spirit. And remember, flexibility is your ally; be willing to adjust your goals in response to life's ebb and flow.

To validate your success, establish clear criteria for each goal. Is it the number of words written, the completion of a draft, or the feedback from a trusted reader? Whatever the measure, let it be a beacon that signals your advance, a confirmation that you are one step closer to your grand aspiration.

Should obstacles arise, as they inevitably do, take heart. Revisit your goals and ask whether they remain relevant and realistic. Consult with fellow writers or mentors who may offer fresh perspectives and solutions. Challenges line the path of a writer, but each one surmounted adds to the strength and luster of your story.

Let these goals be your companions, your rallying cries in the quiet hours of creation. For it is in the setting of these goals that your book begins to breathe, to stir, to rise from the depths of your imagination into the light of day.

FINDING WHAT WORKS FOR YOU

Every writer is an individual and their writing habits are as individual as they are. It is important to have those habits. Figure out what works for you and then stick with it.

The first thing to consider is just how much time you can devote to your writing. If you're thinking in terms of "I'll write when I can," you'll find that doesn't work. There are always things in life which will take the time that you intend to use for writing. Just how many times do you think you can say to yourself, "I'll write tomorrow," before you stop trying to write?

Every committed writer has a regular schedule for their writing. Granted, those best-selling authors living off the royalties of their books don't have to fit writing and working a full-time job into their schedule. But that doesn't mean their schedule is empty; they've got a lot of other things to do, especially when it comes to marketing their books, which takes time away from writing.

How much time you can set aside for writing is up to you and your schedule. For most new writers, a minimum of one hour per day is necessary. Two hours is usually a good top-end for new writers, but some people can write effectively as much as four hours per day. There are also those who choose to write fifteen minutes a day but surprise themselves when it becomes hours. The time you choose will be personal as you build writing habits.

Besides dedicating time to writing, you're going to have to find some place to write. Again, this is a highly personal thing. Most people need quiet, without interruption, to write. So, while a coffee shop may be a good place for checking your e-mail and meeting with people, it might not be a good place for writing.

When I started writing, I needed absolute quiet time before I could get the first sentence. Now, I welcome the sound of the birds outside my window or the dull chatter in the coffee shop.

Discipline Your Time

Not everyone can write seven days a week; I get that. But you should write at least five days a week, even if it is only fifteen minutes per day. Make it a regular time, so that you can get used to the habit of using that time for writing. While there may be things that cause you to skip a writing session one day, guard that time and value it as you value your goal of finishing the book. Unless it is something as important as a doctor's appointment, don't break your appointment to write.

Logging that time and what you accomplish during it is a great way to keep yourself on track. Write the actual time spent writing each day and what you accomplish during that time, such as how many words you wrote. Looking back at this will help you see how well you are doing and may even give you some insight into changes that you need to make to write more efficiently.

Give Yourself Some Accountability

If you really want to accomplish something in life, don't keep it a secret. You can decide you're going to write a book, establish a schedule with due dates for your various steps, and get started, but if you keep what you're doing quiet, you may convince yourself that any slip in the schedule is alright. You can do that repeatedly until you finally give up on the book.

On the other hand, if you tell one good friend that you are writing a book and your schedule for completion, you've suddenly made yourself accountable. You won't want to look bad by telling them you didn't get your chapter done for the week or two weeks; that would make you feel horrible. Accountability alone will drive you to push yourself, helping you meet your goals.

You can take an even bigger step in accountability by posting on social media that you're writing a book. That increases the circle of people who you can make yourself accountable to. Not only that, but it will also give you a great circle of beta readers you can call on when the time comes.

Don't get scared. It's natural to think that posting such plans on social media will get you a lot of negative feedback; but the opposite is true. Your family and friends will become your cheerleaders, especially as you post your progress and on how much you've accomplished.

Refine Your Process

As you write, you'll learn about yourself as a writer. That means learning what works for you. Don't be afraid to change your writing process if you find that what you're doing doesn't work. Maybe the place you've chosen has too many distractions. Maybe you need some quiet instrumental music in the background to relax you so that you can write. You may even find that you need to pick another time in the day, because the time you have chosen has too many interruptions.

Don't be too quick to change, though, just because something doesn't seem to work. Give yourself enough time with that place or schedule so that you can become accustomed to it. Sometimes, it doesn't work, just because it is new.

You need to recognize when something really isn't working, after you've done it long enough for an adequate test. The balance between these two is tricky to find and is ever-changing. Don't change just to change; do so with a purpose.

More than anything, you need to keep yourself on track. That means not allowing other things or other projects to distract you. If you get an idea for another book, write it down; but don't allow yourself to jump from project to project just yet. Stay focused.

STEP 5 WRITING EXERCISE

- Define your project parameters: page number/ word count goal
- Create specific but realistic goals: outline, research, first draft, revise, edit, revise, edit . . . repeat
- Set time limits on each goal: be kind to yourself and remember, life happens
- Create a full timeline that includes writing and editing with space for marketing strategy goals

BUILD YOUR STORY OUTLINE

"The outline is 95 percent of the book. Then I sit down and write, and that's the easy part."–Jeffery Deaver

You're probably thinking by now, *When am I going to write this thing? All I've done is plan and research.* Read Jeffery Deaver's quote again. Your book needs meticulous organization and planning, which we've walked through in Steps 1-5 and now the fun begins.

A story outline is the most useful tool that can ease the writing process, giving your thoughts shape and focus; it serves as the framework for your book, assisting you in visualizing the general organization and content flow. By building an outline that directs your writing and keeps you from becoming lost or overwhelmed by highlighting the important chapters, parts, or ideas, you can approach each chapter of your book with assurance and purpose.

An outline also improves your capacity for coherent cognition and idea organization. Your overview of logical flow of information ensures the narrative develops in a clear and interesting way. Summarizing the dominant themes, subtopics, or significant arguments for each chapter shines a light on holes in your story or development issues.

STRUCTURING THE OUTLINE

Here are some tips to consider when structuring the chapter-by-chapter outline for your book:

1. **Shape the outline around plot development:** If you're creating fiction, think about how the chapters advance the larger storyline; each chapter expanding on the one before it, furthering the plot or introducing fresh ideas. Consider how personal stories or ideas flow in nonfiction and how each chapter advances the dominant theme as well.

2. **Have a specific goal/main idea for each chapter:** Each chapter's aim should be clear. What do you hope to achieve or communicate to the reader? Setting an obvious message or core theme for each chapter can help you stay on task and will give your chapters a sense of purpose.

3. **What is the major action in the chapter:** A gripping scene to draw readers in, making them curious and eager to read further. You can capture readers' attention and establish the chapter's tone by opening with action.

4. **Focus on a key change/pivot in each chapter:** Note the most important development or momentous

happening in each chapter. This could be a character shift, the disclosure of new knowledge, a turning point in the plot, the making of a significant choice, or the completion of a hard task. This keeps your chapters lively and guarantees that your book progresses and develops.

5. **The point isn't to draft your book, but to give direction**: Keep in mind that the chapter-by-chapter plan is a guide to provide structure for the direction of the first draft of your work. It keeps you organized and gives a roadmap for what each chapter entails. Keep your outline succinct and concentrate on summarizing each chapter.

   Fully developing a chapter-by-chapter outline defines your story, establishes clear goals, engages readers with action, includes major changes, and gives your content a clear direction by using the above techniques.

6. **Table of Contents:** When crafting your outline, keep in mind this will often become your Table of Contents. Keep that in mind when working on your Writing Exercise for this chapter.

NOTES ON OUTLINING NONFICTION

With a nonfiction book that is a narrative, like a memoir, creating an outline is just like it is for fiction; but what about other nonfiction books? They can be more challenging, because the order in which information flows often must follow a logical progression, with one piece of information building upon the previous. The reader may not understand the subject being presented if they lack a key piece of information or if items happen out of order.

One of the easiest errors made by authors of these nonfiction works is assuming readers know information the author deems "common knowledge" in a field of expertise. It is often necessary to provide very basic, foundational information to the reader, even if you think they know it. Abbreviations or acronyms should follow the definition in parentheses, i.e., Department of Defense (DOD), usually done the first time it appears in the text followed by only the acronym in subsequent copy.

STEP 6 WRITING EXERCISE

Once you have the basic outline done of the story structure, consider adding the following additional information before creating your first draft.

Chapter Titles: Depending on the genre, adding chapter titles creates another level of connection and communication of your story to the reader.

Chapter Description: Add an overview of each chapter which will keep focus on the key takeaway

Theme: Supporting the description, highlight the theme of the chapter

Additional content: Add any research, materials, or narratives you want to incorporate

Transitions or Flashbacks: How will you segue into each chapter or draw upon previous chapters to support this chapter?

WRITE YOUR FIRST DRAFT

"Get it down. Take chances. It may be bad, but it's the only way you can do anything really good."–William Faulkner

Starting a writing project can be an exciting yet intimidating experience, especially when finally starting the official first draft. The first attempt putting thoughts on paper frequently poses an unanticipated obstacle: self-doubt. A writer often struggles with the uncertainty of their ability to turn ideas into their dream story.

TIPS FOR "GETTING IT DOWN"

Don't worry about writing quality

It's essential to let go of the endless demand for perfection when composing your initial draft. Instead of worrying about every word or sentence, the first step is to get your ideas written on paper. Unleash your imagination to allow yourself to write without inhibition. This freedom will let you experiment with your writing style, explore new ideas, and find gems that would not have been obvious if you had been overly concerned with quality from the outset. Always keep in mind that writing begins with a first draft and that subsequent revisions and polishing will come later.

Only write during your scheduled writing sessions
Scheduling specific writing times might help you stay consistent with writing. By setting aside certain periods to write, you can train your mind to concentrate on the current activity; it helps remove distractions and guarantees that you routinely make progress on your first draft. To gain momentum and get through the initial challenge, consistency is essential. Everyone has their own schedules and productivity habits, so it's crucial to create a writing plan that suits your lifestyle.

You don't have to write in order
Writing in a non-sequential manner is one of the liberating qualities of drafting. You don't have to start at chapter one and write from beginning to end. Plunge in and write about a scenario or idea that inspires you without worrying about the chapter order. You can avoid potential writer's block and keep your creative juices flowing by writing in random order. You can reorganize and connect the various elements to form a coherent narrative later.

Don't let imposter syndrome take over
Accept flaws and write with inhibition, knowing that fixing mistakes and improving your work comes in later drafts. Foster a friendly and encouraging environment for your creativity to develop while ignoring your inner critic.

Track your progress
As you write your first draft, keep track of your progress to inspire and give you a sense of accomplishment. Consult your timeline and goal setting from Step 5.

Your story is *your* world
Imagine the characters, their settings, and their feelings at that moment. You may add authenticity and depth to your work by being emotionally immersed in it. Allow yourself to become swept up in the story, living it with the characters, even if the main character is you–experience it all again. Your initial draft will be of higher quality because of this immersive technique, which also makes the writing process more gratifying, therapeutic, and fun.

Don't get bogged down by descriptions
It's easy to drown in the specifics by taking too much time discussing every aspect of your plot or location. Focusing on them now can impede your progress. Vivid descriptions can improve the reader's experience, but in the first draft, concentrate on outlining the major concepts and plot points. Allow your imagination to soar without obsessing over the "right" words or accurately describing the minutiae of each scene. Accept the idea of a rough draft, which concentrates on concepts and story development without overly detailed explanations.

Forget about fixating on themes for now
Themes are the underlying ideas or meanings that give a literary work depth and purpose. While focusing on topics during your first draft can be daunting, they are necessary for a well-written piece of work. Allow the story to develop spontaneously at this early stage

without feeling obligated to include any specific themes. Put more effort into capturing the soul of your cast of characters, their interactions, and the plot's progression. Engrossing yourself in the story allows the concepts to come naturally into focus.

Once finishing your initial draft, you may go back and analyze the ideas and motifs that come up, turning them into themes during the editing phase. Trust in your storytelling instincts and let the themes reveal themselves as your writing evolves.

Be flexible with the outline you've created
Outlines act as roadmaps, giving your writing process structure and direction. However, it is vital to be open to the prospect of departing from your basic plan when working on the first draft. As your characters and story come to life on the page, new concepts and plot twists might easily occur because writing creates unexpected turns. Accept these unplanned inspirations and be open to changing your plan if necessary. Let your imagination lead you, even if it means deviating from the initial outline. This adaptability might cause fascinating discoveries and unforeseen plot twists that give your work fresh energy. Give yourself the freedom to stray if it advances the plot.

Writing, in its essence, is an act of revealing oneself to the unknown, a leap of faith, a commitment to complete the journey. Are you prepared to commit to the craft, to embrace the mundane of routine? Will you choose to dedicate yourself to the discipline of goals you set?

Let each day be a steppingstone, each paragraph a victory. With each sentence crafted, remind yourself of the honor it is to create worlds with words. And when the path seems arduous and the end distant, remember it is not the mountains ahead that wear you out, but the pebble in your shoe. Take off your shoe, get rid of that pebble, and write on. The world awaits the stories only you can tell.

Now, let's delve into the detailed steps of this process:

The Opening: Your story's beginning should be inviting and powerful. Many readers will judge your book by the first thirty pages; if you don't pique interest immediately, your book heads to the donation pile.

Character Development: Now is the time your character profiles and research come into play. Think of the adage "show, don't tell." Instead of stating that a character is anxious, describe their jittery hands or the way they pace a room—let your readers feel the anxiety.

Plot Progression: Using your outline's plot points, create scenes that not only connect these points but also provide a journey that is both compelling and inevitable. A well-paced plot is like a symphony, with moments of crescendo and decrescendo that engage your readers' emotions.

Dialogue: Dialogue is the rhythm of your prose and the pulse of your narrative. A well-timed one-liner can underscore a crucial moment, much like a single beam of light can illuminate a darkened room. Where appropriate, let the voices of your characters ring out through authentic dialogue, adding texture and depth to your creation.

Sensory Details: Engage all five senses to immerse your readers in the environment. The rustle of leaves, the tang of citrus, the scratch of wool—such details bring a scene to vibrant life.

DEALING WITH WRITER'S BLOCK

In the world of writing, the blank page is both a canvas of endless possibilities and, paradoxically, an imposing wall that can halt a writer's progress. As we venture deeper into the craft of writing a book, we arrive at a phenomenon known in hushed tones amongst authors as *writer's block*. It looms over the creative process, a formidable barrier that can zap the momentum from even the most seasoned writer.

Writer's block is not a mere inconvenience—it is a force that can derail months of work, causing distress and doubt in its wake. The ramifications of this creative impasse are not to be underestimated. If left unchecked, the block can turn into a prolonged absence from writing, eroding confidence, and perhaps leaving a once-promising book to gather dust, unfinished and forgotten.

But fear not, for this challenge is not insurmountable. There is a beacon of hope, a strategy that serves as a key to unlock the chains of writer's block; one must embrace the art of writing poorly. Yes, you read that correctly—to write poorly, at least in the beginning. Give yourself the permission to draft without judgment, to let the words flow without critiquing every phrase. This is the draft's purpose: to be molded and sculpted into refinement through subsequent revisions.

When the well of inspiration runs dry, draw from different sources. Go back to your notes from Steps 1, 2, and 3 to connect back to your why of writing the story and who you are writing for. Many times, when you are reminded of the core purpose of your story, you'll be able to get out of your head and back to writing for your reader.

You can also get your muse's attention by reading, especially those outside of your usual genre, watching films, listening to music, or delving into the visual arts. Creativity is often a response to the work of others, a dialogue between your voice and the voices who came before.

In moments where the words refuse to come, step away from your writing space. Engage in different activities that occupy the hands but frees the mind—cooking, gardening, cleaning, or even a hot shower. These tasks allow the subconscious to work through narrative knots, often leading to breakthroughs upon returning to the manuscript.

Should the block persist, reach out to fellow writers or trusted readers. Discussing your work can shine a new light on old problems, providing fresh perspectives or the encouragement needed to push forward. Sometimes, the small act of verbalizing your ideas unravels the complexities that have left you stymied.

Let us not forget the power of routine. Consistency breeds habit, and habit can coax the muse out of hiding. Dedicate a specific time each day to writing and honor it as a sacred appointment. Over time, the mind learns to switch into writing mode during these periods, easing the transition from thought to expression.

Amidst these methods, it is crucial to maintain self-compassion. Acknowledge that writer's block is a common struggle, not a personal failure. It afflicts novice and expert alike. With patience and perseverance, writer's block dissipates.

In summary, while writer's block is a formidable adversary, it is not invincible. Through a combination of tactical approaches—embracing imperfection, setting modest goals, changing environments, seeking inspiration, stepping away, engaging others, establishing routine, freewriting, and practicing self-kindness—you can dismantle the barriers that impede your progress.

The Importance of Empathy
Empathy, the ability to understand and share the feelings of another, is paramount. This emotional exchange breathes life into characters and imbues narratives with a soul. Relatability connects the dots between the fictional and the real, allowing readers to see a part of themselves reflected in the pages. The audience experiences inform reader interpretation and must be considered when writing. Perception, the act of processing and understanding, ultimately determines the impact of the written word.

Empathy, then, is not just a word but a gateway to the hearts of your readers. It is the silent whisper of shared humanity that echoes in the chambers of the soul, binding author and audience, in a dance as old as storytelling itself.

How does one evoke empathy within prose? Through characters that are flawed yet striving, through trials that are arduous yet surmountable, and through victories that, while often small, are deeply satisfying.

STEP 7 WRITING EXERCISE

Create your first draft without self-editing. Yes, it will be harder than you expect, but you can do it!

TAKE A BREAK

"When you write a book, you spend day after day scanning and identifying the trees. When you're done, you have to step back and look at the forest."—Stephen King

A creative work's first draft is an enormous accomplishment. It results from endless hours, a storm of thoughts, and a relentless need to put ideas into words. You might feel a wave of success and relief as you put down the literal or metaphorical pen. However, this accomplishment hides a seductive impulse to dive right into the freshly written draft and start reading and dissecting every word. This need is natural and results from a desire to evaluate the caliber of your work and look for recognition for your efforts. However, avoiding this temptation is beneficial for your creative endeavors. In this chapter, we'll address the reasons waiting to read through the first draft is crucial, examine the dangers of not waiting, and provide suggestions for how taking a break can encourage development, objectivity, and ultimately the possibility of a more polished final product.

THE PSYCHOLOGY OF A BREAK

In the relentless pursuit of the written word, authors often find themselves tangled in a web of their own narratives. It is in these moments that the wisdom of stepping away, of taking a break, becomes not just beneficial but necessary for the craft.

When immersed in creating a manuscript, the writer often becomes too close to the project–like not seeing the forest for the trees. The problem at hand is not just potential for writer's block, but a myriad of subtle issues that can arise when forcing yourself to keep writing after the first draft is done: stale prose, plot inconsistencies or holes, underdeveloped characters, and superfluous narrative. Frustration and fatigue might not just mar the quality of writing but also affect an author's relationship with their work, sometimes resulting in a deep-seated aversion to finish any ongoing projects.

So, what solves this pervasive challenge? It lies in the psychology of a break. Taking deliberate time away from the manuscript allows the mind to reset and refresh, providing a new perspective upon return. This is not about abandoning the work but enriching it through strategic retreat.

An author might schedule regular breaks, stepping away from the manuscript after a set amount of time or upon reaching certain milestones. These breaks can take many forms: a walk in nature, a change of scenery, or engaging in a different creative activity. The key is to create mental space from the work.

In a world saturated with words and a constant push for productivity, consider this: a well-timed pause might be the most productive act of all. Can you recall when stepping back granted you clarity? Breaks are not a sign of weakness, but a strategic tool for strength. They offer a respite where the mind can wander, unhindered by the immediate demands of syntax and structure. And in that wandering, there is wonder to be found.

In the end, the psychology of a break is about honoring the ebb and flow of creativity.

FIVE MORE REASONS TO TAKE A BREAK

1. **Give your body and brain a break**
   It can be physically and mentally taxing to write. Get a massage, take up yoga or long walks in nature. Rejuvenate your senses.

2. **Prevent writer's block**
   It is intimidating to read through your first draft right away after finishing it. Writer's block may result from the critical voice in your head ripping apart each sentence and doubting your decisions, causing crippling self-doubt. Give yourself a chance to remove yourself emotionally from the initial writing process by delaying the evaluation. This psychological detachment lessens the strain of self-criticism, enabling you to approach the editing process with newfound creativity and clarity.

3. **Allow yourself to edit with a fresh set of eyes**
   Reading the first draft right away after it's finished can lead to tunnel vision. If you spend too much time with the content, you can miss plot holes, weak points, or structural problems. You get a new perspective by pausing for a while and coming

back to your draft later. By approaching the revision process with a more critical and objective eye, you can identify areas that need improvement, improve the coherence of your work, and produce a top-notch book.

4. **To get a better sense of the overall direction for your book**
Writing the first draft is like beginning a journey without a precise map. Characters grow naturally during this exploratory process, where ideas may flow freely. Give the story time to settle and the themes will become clear, and you'll get a better understanding of the overall direction. You can evaluate the draft's advantages and disadvantages, note narrative arcs, and determine whether the plot conforms to your original intent. This larger viewpoint aids in your decision-making during the revision process, resulting in a more coherent and focused text.

5. **Allow new ideas to seep in**
Creativity is an ever-changing and developing energy. Allowing oneself time away from the first draft creates room for fresh insights to emerge. You might discover new ideas, interesting viewpoints, or creative story twists when you get involved in other pursuits or expose yourself to various sources of inspiration.

Give yourself ample time before looking at your first draft
This period varies from writer to writer, from a week to even a month, and allows for mental rest and renewal,

offering ample separation from the initial writing process. You will have plenty of time to devote to other elements of your life, learn new things, and approach your work with a new perspective. Following this break, you will come back to your draft with renewed vigor and a fresh outlook, prepared to attack the editing process with greater objectivity and originality.

WHAT TO DO ON YOUR FIRST DRAFT BREAK

Much like a Spring Break of the mind, think of this as a mini vacation of sorts. Here are a few suggestions, but feel free to add to the list.

The writing journey is not linear. It is within these spaces that we can harness the power of productive distancing—a paradoxical concept that involves stepping back to leap forward. What follows is a guide to making the most out of breaks without losing touch with the essence of your project.

Let's embark on a journey of exploration, where we uncover the intricacies of productive distancing. We will delve into a list of strategies designed to help you maximize your break periods, ensuring that when you return to your project, your mind rejuvenates, and your narrative enriched.

Scheduled reflection

To begin our deep dive, let's explore the practice of scheduled reflection. This involves setting aside specific times to step away and ponder your work from a distance. Not unlike an artist stepping back from their canvas, this practice allows you to see the broader strokes of your narrative.

This strategic retreat is not about idle time. It is about engaging in a silent dialogue with your work. Ask yourself: What are the overarching themes? Are the character arcs evolving? What is the heart of the story? These questions can lead to revelations that are often obscured by the proximity of constant writing.

To support this approach, a study published in the *Journal of Applied Psychology* found that structured time for reflection led to improved performance in subsequent tasks. Writers who have employed scheduled reflection often report breakthroughs that might have remained elusive amidst the rigors of continuous writing.

Take a break completely from writing

Physical rejuvenation is a critical element of productive distancing. It involves taking time to care for your body—through exercise, rest, or even simply stepping outside for fresh air.

Exercise can be essential for writers. It not only benefits physical health, but also mental acuity. Incorporate activities like yoga, running, or even a leisurely walk into your breaks. These actions not only provide a physical reset but also offer the opportunity for your mind to wander, often leading to unexpected creative insights.

Read for enjoyment

During your breaks, immerse yourself in the works and wisdom of talented authors. This is not about imitation, but about understanding the principles that underpin their craft and enjoying their mastery.

Talk about your story ideas with friends and peers
Finally, do not underestimate the value of social interaction and networking. Engaging with fellow writers and enthusiasts can provide moral support, fresh ideas, and constructive criticism. This interaction is a breeding ground for creativity and motivation.

By sharing your experiences and listening to others, you can gain new perspectives on your work. The relationships you build during these interactions can lead to collaborative opportunities and a sense of community–attend writing workshops, join book clubs, or take part in online writing forums.

Think about your marketing strategy and launch plan
Create a timeline for your marketing and launching your book (even if you have not made your decision on how to publish). You will need an author website and some sort of social media presence. Starting now will allow you to interact with potential readers and build excitement about your book before it's even written.

Take a trip into the mind of your reader. Put yourself in their shoes for a day.
Getting back in touch with your target reader will allow you to approach your next edit with them fresh in your mind.

STEP 8 WRITING EXERCISE

In the relentless pursuit of writing your story, a poignant reality confronts every wordsmith: the well of ingenuity risks running dry. How, then, can one circumvent this looming specter of creative exhaustion? The answer lies in unplugging to recharge.

So, instead of writing for this step's exercise, I challenge you to sit and daydream about your story. Go through it like a movie in your mind, not for critique, but only for enjoyment.

If this brings you any type of stress, switch your daydream to imagining yourself perhaps on vacation and being recognized as the author of your award-winning book.

Have fun with this exercise. You have earned this break and need to remember that, because the next step may be even tougher than writing.

REVISIT, REVISE, AND EDIT, *OH MY!*

"After writing and before publishing a book, the writer should read it as a reader since such insight mirrors the flaws."—Ehsan Sehgal

Revisiting Your Manuscript

As a writer, returning to your manuscript after a period of separation can be both exhilarating and intimidating. This chapter will guide you through this critical phase, providing a strategic approach to refine your work, ensuring your vision communicates clarity and has an impact.

There are common misconceptions regarding this stage of writing. Some believe that a first draft should be near perfect and require minimal revision. This is a fallacy that can hinder a writer's progress. The first draft is not the end, but the beginning of the journey to a finished book.

Please approach this process with patience, focus, and a few essential tools: your manuscript, a comfortable workspace, a note-taking device (whether digital or traditional), and an open mind.

Read Through and Take Notes

The first step is to read your draft in its entirety, making no changes. This allows you to experience the story as a reader and identify overarching issues. Ask yourself, does the narrative arc compel the reader to read on? Are the characters' motivations clear and their actions consistent? Is the pacing balanced, or are there sections that drag or rush?

Reading the first draft aloud will also help bring to light any awkward sections. You may need to set aside a few days to do this. Make notes as to sticky sections to come back to, but do not make edits at this time; this is an exploration to find those areas to refine. Pay close attention to the plot's development, the concepts' coherence, and the reader's experience.

Be vigilant for common pitfalls: overly descriptive passages that stall the narrative, dialogue that sounds unnatural, or inconsistencies in character behavior. Look for subtle threads that may need to be woven back into the tapestry of the story or trimmed for good.

Organize Your Notes into Different Categories

Organize your ideas and notes into distinct categories after you've finished your initial read-through and note-taking.

Establish subcategories for "Issues in the story," "Problems within a particular section," "Continuity problems," and "Minor miscellaneous problems." You will get a clearer picture of the problems and topics that need to be addressed during the editing process, thanks to this categorization. Make sure you note specifically what chapters or page numbers the problems lie when categorizing them.

Should you encounter the frustration of a stubborn chapter or a scene that refuses to come together, step back. Troubleshooting is an art in itself. Ask yourself: Is this scene necessary? Are my characters acting true to form? Sometimes, the solution is not more editing but the courage to cut what no longer fits.

Consider the opening of your book—does it immediately hook the reader? A compelling start is a promise to your audience of the journey to come. As you revisit your introduction, ensure it's not just informative but impossible to put down.

Balance is key in your language. Employ vivid imagery to transport your reader but temper it with simplicity. For example, a sunset need not always be "a symphony of colors dancing in the sky"; sometimes, it is enough to say, "the sun melted into the horizon". The power of a well-placed verb can outshine a clutter of adjectives.

Remember, rhythm and cadence are the heartbeat of storytelling. A sentence can be a soft whisper or a thunderclap—it's in the arrangement of words, the weaving of long and short, the pause and the rush. When you find the perfect dialogue, let it breathe on the page. A line of conversation can reveal more about a character than paragraphs of description. It's not just what is said but the silences in between—the unspoken words that resonate with the truth.

And to repeat the phrase again: show, don't tell. Rather than telling the reader of a character's despair, show the crumpled photo clutched in trembling hands, the gaze lingering on a vacant chair, the silence that now fills a room once filled with laughter.

Often, the simplest expression is the most powerful.

Editing

Let's discuss how editing takes your story to the next level.

1. Clarify and organize ideas to present a narrative that is understandable, memorable, and well-structured.
2. Checks for consistency and coherence to ensure logical connections, correcting any errors, and inconsistency in character voice or settings.
3. "Gets to the verb" to enhance conciseness by communicating ideas in the simplest and clearest way possible.
4. Polishes the overall presentation looking for structural issues, style, spelling, and grammar.

Editing Checklist

There are a lot of things you should look at as you review and revise your rough draft. This is where the rubber hits the road, and you prove your ability as a writer. How well you can self-edit will determine whether anyone else takes your work seriously, so you'd better take it seriously before they even see it.

On the positive side, this is your opportunity to really shine. As you tighten up your story line, find the things you missed saying to make sure the story holds the reader's interest. Anyone can write a rough draft but turning that into a quality book takes work. The following checklist prompts will give you things to look for. I've broken it down into sections to make it more manageable.

Your Story Line

- Does your story resonate with the reader? Is it good?

- Is your protagonist likeable, interesting, and believable?
- Does your protagonist grow adequately through the story and do you explain effectively what causes them to grow?
- Is the situation the protagonist must overcome, compelling?
- Do you have a strong opening, hitting the five Ws (who, what, where, when, and why)?
- Is the story paced well, rising and falling for interest?
- Is the ending of the story satisfying, leaving the reader feeling good?
- Do the scenes follow a logical progression?
- Do all the scenes contribute directly to enhancing the plot?

Your Writing Style

- Do you maintain a consistent point of view throughout the story?
- Are you consistent in your use of tense (past, present, and future), except where that might change in the story (going back to the past in a flashback)?
- Did you go overboard with your use of adjectives? (If so, you can eliminate them by using stronger nouns)
- Can you replace adverbs with stronger verbs?
- Is your dialog believable and easy to follow?
- Have you properly used metaphors, similes, and any cliches?
- Is your writing style consistent, maintaining the same voice?
- Is the "voice" for each character consistent throughout the story?

- Are you using an active voice throughout?
- Have you eliminated any awkward sentences that are easy to stumble over?
- Is my tone appropriate for the subject and audience?

Technical Aspects of Writing
- Have you inspected your grammar, specifically punctuation?
- Have you used a grammar checker to verify the proper use of challenging words?
- Is it easy to follow conversations without losing track of who is talking?
- Did you eliminate repetitive words?
- Have you given credit to other works that you have drawn from and are any citations correctly formatted?

PROFESSIONAL EDITING

Developmental Edit
This is the first and arguably the most transformative stage of editing. Here, the manuscript is dissected at its core. We examine the overarching themes, plot structure, and character development. A developmental editor acts as an architect, analyzing the blueprint of your narrative and identifying areas where the foundation may need reinforcement or redesign.

The developmental editor delves into the heart of your story, questioning the motivations of your characters and the believability of their arcs. They probe the plot for holes that may trip the reader and suggest ways to weave subplots into the main narrative tapestry. Is your antagonist's transformation believable? Does the climax leave the reader breathless with satisfaction, or does it need more buildup?

Credible sources, such as esteemed writing coaches and successful authors, vouch for the importance of this stage. Renowned author Stephen King, in his memoir *On Writing*, underscores the need for a writer to be open to significant changes and drastic improvements during developmental editing.

In practical applications, developmental editing might involve reordering chapters to enhance suspense, deepening character backstories, or even changing the point of view to better serve the story. This phase is about seeing the forest for the trees, ensuring that the story flows seamlessly from beginning to end.

Line Edit

Once the structure stands firm, we turn to line editing. Line editors scrutinize each sentence, looking for inconsistencies in tone, overused phrases, and awkward constructions. They enhance the rhythm and flow of your writing, ensuring that each word carries weight and contributes to the overarching narrative.

Testimonials from authors who have had their work transformed by a keen editorial eye provide evidence of the power of a line edit. They speak of clunky sentences turned elegant and dialogue that once fell flat now crackling with tension.

For practical applications, consider how a line editor might suggest a more powerful verb to replace a weak one, or how they might break up a lengthy, convoluted sentence into two that are clear and concise.

Copy Edit

Copy editors are the gatekeepers of clarity, precision, and consistency. They maintain your voice while ensuring that technical errors do not distract the reader. They are the last line of defense against blatant errors that can undermine the credibility of your work. Copy editing ensures that your book adheres to style guides, that timelines are consistent, and that information is accurate.

Proofreader

Even though you have painstakingly polished your book through one or several editors, the last pass should always be with a proofreader. And I offer you this Pro Tip: Always proofread your book from a physical copy, not on screen. It's amazing how many errors are missed because our brain and eye coordination "fix" common typos and incorrect words. It is also best to not only hire a pro but also proofread this yourself from a book copy and ask a friend or family member who is an avid reader to help as well. It's the last sweep that ensures your book is ready to face the scrutiny of advance readers.

Here's a personal story to reiterate the importance of proofreading:

> We had just published a fantastic alternative history novel after at least three proofread passes by five people. The book had been out about a month when my oldest brother picked up a copy I had brought along to our family reunion. He's an avid reader, and I was happy to see him enjoying the story.

About half-way through, he looked up and said the dreaded phrase, "I found a typo."

"What? Where?" My heart sunk into my stomach. I literally could not believe after all the passes and eyes that looked it over that there could indeed be a mistake (and yes, I AM a bit of a perfectionist).

Then he clarified, "Well, not a typo per se. It's the wrong word."

OOOOF! Gut punch. It seems sometimes even proofreaders, authors, and publishers get too involved in a good story and their minds read the word that should be there, as opposed to what IS there. In this example, our villain reached for an anecdote instead of the antidote ... perhaps that's why he died (insert snicker here).

As we transition from one editing stage to another, we must remember that each serves a distinct and crucial role in the evolution of a manuscript. The developmental edit constructs the skeleton, the line edit adds flesh and muscle, the copy edit smooths the skin, and the proofread swaddles this body of work like a comfy blanket ready for the world to embrace.

SELF-EDITING VS. PROFESSIONAL EDITING

Creativity marks the journey of writing but so does the meticulous refinement of the manuscript. However, each type of editing carries distinct advantages and challenges, and the choice between them can significantly impact the quality and reception of your work.

The craft of self-editing is an introspective voyage where the writer becomes their own critic. It requires a disciplined eye and a willingness to question one's own work. The self-editing author must oscillate between creator and editor, often leading to new insights and improvements that maintain the authenticity of the original voice. This path allows for a deeply personal final manuscript, shaped entirely by the author's vision.

In contrast, professional editing brings an external perspective to the table. A professional editor serves as an objective arbiter of quality, providing expertise that can elevate a manuscript to professional standards. They come armed with industry knowledge and a detachment from the text that can identify issues the author might overlook.

When comparing these two editing approaches, several criteria stand out. The richness of the manuscript, the clarity of expression, adherence to grammatical standards, and the flow of the narrative are all aspects that are scrutinized during the editing process.

In terms of similarities, both self-editing and professional editing strive to achieve a coherent, engaging narrative. Each process involves examining the text for language consistency, narrative structure, and character development. Regardless of who wields the red pen, the goal remains the same: to refine the manuscript until it shines.

Yet, the differences are telling. Self-editing is more budget-friendly and allows the writer to retain full control over the creative process. However, it may lack the objectivity necessary to catch all errors and plot inconsistencies. Writers are often too close to their work to see the flaws, leading to missed opportunities for improvement. Remember the forest for the trees analogy?

Professional editing, while requiring financial investment, brings a level of polish and expertise that is hard to match. Professional editors can spot the subtle nuances that need tweaking and have the skills to fix them.

Analyzing these editing paths reveals broader implications. In the age of self-publishing, the debate between self-editing and professional editing has never been more relevant. As the market becomes increasingly saturated, the importance of a well-edited book that stands out for its quality is imperative.

Consider the practical implications. A novel filled with errors, no matter how captivating its story, risks being dismissed by readers and critics alike. Conversely, a meticulously edited book reflects professionalism and respect for the reader, which can translate into better reviews, higher sales, and a more robust author reputation.

A good standard is to do your own self-editing up to where you think your manuscript is the best you can make it, then pass it along to a professional editor. It truly is the difference between a good book and a great one. Also, make sure the editor you choose is familiar with the genre of your story; this is very important because there are certain standards and tropes that readers look for in genres like fantasy, romance, thrillers, as well as memoir, self-help, and business books.

STEP 9 EXERCISE

You've done the work. You've taken a break and made notes. It's time to start your self-edit.

Now is also a good time to research a professional editor if you choose. Remember, find an editor who is familiar with your genre and decide what type of editor you will need, developmental, line, or copy editor.

STEP 10

GET FEEDBACK

"If I waited for perfection, I would never write a word."—Margaret Atwood

I t's critical to understand the value of gathering feedback as you begin the creative path of writing stories, books, novels, etc. Feedback is an essential link between the author and their audience because writing success depends on connection and communication. Whether you're new to writing or an aspiring author, seeking and accepting comments can improve your writing evolution. It offers viewpoints that may elevate your craft to new heights, delivers priceless insights, and identifies blind spots.

The goal is precise: to refine your manuscript through the eyes of external perspectives. This process will not only illuminate the strengths and weaknesses of your work, but also provide you with the invaluable insight necessary to elevate your story from good to exceptional.

- When to Get Feedback
- After the First Draft
- After you have exhausted your own self-editing

- Do not ask for feedback before you have confidence in your story
- When you feel stuck
- After every major revision or edit you make

Feedback acts to support and enhance your creative vision and voice rather than to replace it. By deliberately timing your feedback requests, outside perspectives can strengthen and polish your writing, creating a piece of work that is both powerful and resonant.

Selecting Beta Readers

Go back to the perfect reader avatar you created when deciding who you were writing this book for. Try to match your beta reader to this person as closely as you can.

Identify the traits of an effective beta reader. Look for individuals who are avid readers with an appreciation for your genre. They should possess the ability to articulate their thoughts clearly and to offer criticism without malice. An ideal beta reader understands the balance between personal preference and elements that support and nurture a book's universal appeal.

By mining your social media lists or building a mailing list from your author website (if you have one), you can query people already connected to you. This will also build a stronger fan base. Reach out to anyone you know who enjoys reading, include family, coworkers, and friends.

Consider your personal and professional networks, writing groups, and online communities. A carefully crafted query can yield a group of volunteers keen to dive into your manuscript. Remember to communicate the commitment involved and the type of feedback you're seeking.

Create guidelines for things you'd like them to pay attention to, such as dialogue, character development, storyline, etc.

When you have assembled your candidates, it's prudent to provide them with a clear framework for their feedback. This could be a questionnaire that probes character development, pacing, and plot, or a more open-ended request for their overall impressions and suggestions.

Remember to always thank your beta readers. Everyone's time is precious, and acknowledgement of their help is mandatory.

Gathering Feedback

Here is the 30,000-foot view of the steps involved in gathering feedback: select your early readers, prepare your manuscript for review, communicate your feedback needs, receive the feedback, and then the crucial part—analyze and integrate the insights you've gathered.

Let's delve deeper into each stage, shall we?

Make sure when selecting your early readers to assemble a diverse ensemble who can each bring a unique perspective to your narrative. Choose individuals who represent a cross-section of your potential audience, and if possible, include at least one professional editor or writer who can provide technical critique.

Preparing your manuscript for review is much like dressing for an important interview. You want your work to be presentable, free of glaring errors that could distract from the substance. Provide a clean, well-formatted copy that invites readers to engage with the content, not the typos.

Guide your readers by asking specific questions about characters, plot coherence, and pacing. Encourage honesty and create a safe space for genuine critique. Remember, sugar-coated feedback, while pleasant, will not help you grow.

Receiving feedback is an exercise in humility and discernment. Not all criticism will be constructive, and not all will align with your vision. Practice the art of listening, truly listening, and resist the urge to defend your work. Gather the feedback with gratitude, for each piece is a steppingstone towards improvement.

Which suggestions resonate with the core of your story? Which critiques reveal a disconnect between your intent and the readers' interpretations? This is where you must be meticulous, separating the wheat from the chaff and using these insights to refine your narrative.

A word of advice: don't rush this process. Let the feedback simmer in your mind, allowing the insights to spark your creative instincts. And beware—the allure of endless revisions can be a rabbit hole. Seek balance, knowing when to incorporate feedback and when to stand firm on your artistic choices.

As for testing the validity of the changes you've made, return to your trusted readers with the revised sections. Do they feel the improvement? Is the narrative's clarity enhanced? Their responses will be the compass that guides your final adjustments.

Should you encounter conflicting feedback, that's OK. Troubleshoot these discrepancies by searching for the underlying issues. Often, contradictory comments can reveal a deeper ambiguity in your writing that, once addressed, will unify your readers' experiences.

As beta readers return their thoughts, analyze the feedback with an objective lens. Look for common threads that might show issues needing attention. It's a delicate dance, discerning which advice to take and which to leave, but it's essential for refining your narrative until it sings.

The evidence of this approach's effectiveness lies in countless testimonies from successful authors who attribute a significant portion of their work's refinement to their beta readers. Their stories underscore the transformative power of a well-chosen critique circle.

In rare cases, an alternative approach might be to hire professional beta readers. While this incurs a cost, it ensures a level of professionalism and expertise that can be invaluable, particularly for new authors.

Selecting beta readers is not merely a task to be checked off; it is an invitation to collaboration, a bridge between the solitude of writing and the chorus of voices who will elevate your book from good to great.

Interpreting Feedback

When deciphering beta reader feedback, a methodical approach is essential. Authors must learn to interpret feedback critically, distinguishing between subjective preference and objective observation. Seeking patterns such as recurring comments are likely indicative of areas in need of attention. It is also vital to consider the source of each piece of feedback; the insights of a fellow writer or a reader well-versed in your genre can hold more weight than those less familiar with the craft or the subject matter.

Implementing this approach involves several steps. Begin by organizing the feedback into categories, such as character development, pacing, plot consistency, and thematic clarity. Within each category, evaluate the comments. Do they offer specific examples or vague impressions? Are they aligned with your vision for the book, or do they steer it in an unwanted direction?

Next, prioritize the feedback. Determine which suggestions will have the greatest impact on improving your manuscript and which to set aside. This process requires honest self-reflection and an openness to change, balanced with the confidence to stand by the core aspects of your work.

The effectiveness of this method is not speculative; the experiences of many successful authors support it. These writers often recount how critical feedback helped to transform their manuscripts from mediocre drafts to polished novels. Their stories serve as evidence that discerning which feedback to incorporate—and how—can make the difference between a book that falters and one that soars.

As you ponder the feedback, let your mind's eye paint a vivid picture of the many possible futures of your story. What if that character's arc took a slightly different trajectory? Could a subtle shift in pacing illuminate a previously hidden theme? Engage with the feedback as you would a conversation with a mentor, full of probing questions and enlightening revelations.

Feedback, when interpreted with care and wisdom, is not an adversary; it is a beacon that, if followed, can lead an author out of the forest and into the light of a book's fullest expression. It is a dance between the writer's intent and the reader's experience, a partnership that, when done well, culminates in a work that is not only written but also truly read.

OVERVIEW (BECAUSE IT BEARS REPEATING)

Dos and Don'ts of Feedback

Dos:

- **Address the major issues first:** By addressing items such as plot structure, character development, or pacing first, you may avoid significant revisions later.
- **Have an Open Mind:** When receiving feedback, keep an open mind. It presents a chance for development and improvement, so consider how various viewpoints fit into the vision for your work.
- **Search for Agreement:** Pay special attention to the same feedback provided by multiple reviewers.
- **Be Clear in Your Request:** Make clear the input you're looking for by indicating whether you need feedback on the conversation, character development, or any other component. This helps your beta readers narrow their criticism and offer more focused insight.
- **Select the Ideal Candidates:** Ask individuals who are in your target audience or are knowledgeable about the genre or topic you're writing. Their opinions will be more pertinent and useful.

Don'ts:

- **Don't Take It Feedback Personally:** It will be hard to separate your story from the feedback, especially if it is a memoir, but you must. View responses as a way to improve the story. You are writing for the reader and their comments are just that, the reader's interpretation.

- **Don't Blindly Accept or Reject Feedback:** Consider the source of the comment. Is this topic the reader's area of expertise? How does the criticism align with your writing objectives? You alone decide whether to take suggestions.
- **Avoid Defensive Reactions:** Resist the urge to act defensively or dismissively; instead, seek explanation and delve further into the criticism to comprehend any underlying issues.
- **Don't Disregard Positive Feedback:** It's important to concentrate on things that need improvement, but it is also important to know what is working and enjoyed by the reader.

BETA READER WORKSHEET

Earlier, I told you to be specific in your ask of your beta readers by providing them with a list of specific questions to answer. The more concise the list of questions you can provide, the greater the chance of receiving the answers you need. However, craft the questionnaire to fit your story specifically.

Opening
- Was the opening compelling, drawing you into the story and making you want to keep reading?
- Did you figure out what was going on quickly? (Please note that you may not want them to figure out what was going on quickly. If that's the case, then ask them when they finally figured out what happened.)

- Did the story continue to hold your interest through the first several chapters, compelling you to continue reading?
- Do you feel the story began in the right place?

Characters
- Were the main characters properly developed or do they need more detail?
- Could you directly relate to the main character?
- Did the protagonist grow adequately throughout the story?
- Were there any secondary characters who you felt needed more development?
- Did the characters seem real?
- Could the antagonist (bad guy) be more interesting? How?
- Was there any confusion in your mind about who was whom in the book?
- Was there good "chemistry" between the main characters?
- Are the relationships between the characters believable?

Plot & Conflict
- Is the conflict the protagonist deals with believable and well-defined?
- Are any secondary conflicts adding or detracting from the overall story?
- Does the story line avoid clichés?
- Are the plot twists believable and unexpected, drawing the reader further into the story?
- Do the characters act in a believable manner to the various problems they face?

- Is there enough tension in the story to make it a "page turner?"
- Were there places where the story dragged?
- Was there anything or anyone unnecessary in the story?
- Did you encounter any discrepancies in time sequence, plot sequence, or location?

Dialogue
- Did the dialogue between the characters sound natural and believable?
- Are characters' "voices" consistent and distinct from each other?
- Is there sufficient dialogue? Is there too much?
- Does the dialogue help to move the story forward or does it slow it down?

Setting & Visualization
- Were you able to "see" the scenes, especially the locations, in your imagination?
- Did the descriptions of the scenes draw you in, helping you to see necessary or interesting details?
- Were you able to "see" the actions of the characters? In action scenes, could you follow them, or did you get lost?
- For action sequences, could you keep track of who was doing what or did you mistake one character for another?
- Could you easily form an image of each character in your mind?

Pacing
- Do the various scenes progress compellingly, drawing the story forward?

- Does every scene or chapter add something to the overall story?
- Are there any spots where the story seems to drag?
- Are there any places where backstory or flashbacks detract from the overall story?

Overall Impression
- Does the writing style fit the story?
- Is the voice unique and interesting?
- Does the story deliver what the introduction promises?
- Is the tone appropriate?
- Is the point of view consistent, other than where changes are intentional?

Ending
- Was the resolution to the final conflict satisfying?
- Was the ending believable?
- Did the protagonist receive adequate resolve in their struggles?

FEEDBACK ETIQUETTE

Imagine a beta reader has pointed out a flaw in your character development that you hadn't noticed. It's a moment of truth—will you become defensive, or will you embrace the opportunity for growth? The most effective response is one of openness and humility. Acknowledge the merit in their observation and share your plans for addressing the issue. In doing so, you transform a potentially uncomfortable conversation into a collaborative effort towards excellence.

Of course, not all feedback will be constructive, and you may encounter critiques that are more subjective than objective. It's essential to approach these comments with diplomacy, acknowledging the reader's experience while gently explaining why you might not incorporate their suggestion. Remember, every reader's experience is valid, but not all advice will serve your story's purpose.

As you navigate the delicate process of receiving and responding to feedback, consider the stories of authors who have come before you. Their experiences often highlight the transformative power of well-handled critique. Their words, woven into your own narrative of the revision and response, remind both you and your readers that the journey to publication is shared.

Remember, publishing your book doesn't end the relationship with your beta readers. Keep them informed about your progress, and when the day comes that your work is bound and gracing bookshelves, offer them a special acknowledgment. Their early belief in your story helped it take flight, and such loyalty and support are invaluable. Mastering the art of feedback etiquette ensures that your journey as a writer is marked by mutual respect, learning, and gratitude—a journey that, with each word of thanks, becomes a little less solitary.

Make sure your beta readers know how grateful you are for their time, and they feel special being one of your chosen few.

STEP 10 WRITING EXERCISE 1

Create your beta reader questionnaire for your book specifically.

STEP 10 WRITING EXERCISE 2

Develop a template for a thank you note to your beta readers. Leave space where you can personalize as much or as little as you'd like, but keeping it as special to the individual as possible.

If you have the means, think of something small but heartfelt you can add to your note. Whether a small coffee gift card or handmade trinket or even just a handwritten note can really make a favorable impression on the beta reader and endear them to the project.

PUBLISHING MODELS

*"Turning a manuscript into a book is easy; getting
the manuscript ready to become a book is hard."*
–A.P. Fuchs

Where should I Publish?
Writing a book is an impressive feat; it takes imagination, commitment, and endless hours of work. However,
it's important for prospective writers to understand that
creating the story is only half the struggle. The process
to publish needs a fresh approach and a plan.

The publishing industry, once an impenetrable for-
tress guarded by gatekeepers, has evolved into a more
diverse landscape, offering traditional, independent,
and self-publishing routes. Each path has its own chan-
nel and guidelines.

Understanding the nuances between publishing
business models empowers writers to make informed
decisions that align with their personal goals, resources, and creative vision. It is important to demystify the
complexities of the industry and reveal each choice
objectively. The publishing model decision affects
not only the author's work but also their brand, their

engagement with readers, and their overall career trajectory.

Let's consider criteria such as control over the creative process, time to market, financial investment, and potential for earning and recognition. These benchmarks will serve as our guide.

When we examine these criteria, similarities between traditional and independent publishing emerge. Both avenues can lead to the same destination—a published book. Each can offer validation, a sense of accomplishment, and the potential to reach an audience. Each also requires the author to be a part of marketing efforts.

Yet, the contrasts are stark and significant. Traditional publishing is usually seen as the preference–the brass ring for authors. This is in part because there is no investment needed from the author. It provides a structured and often rigorous vetting process after a successful agent's pitch, with a level of perceived prestige and professionalism. Authors may receive an advance against royalties, gain benefit from the expertise of seasoned editors and designers, and be granted access to wider distribution channels. However, this comes at the cost of relinquishing degrees of creative control and a longer journey from manuscript to bookshelf.

In contrast, independent publishing—whether through small traditional presses, hybrid publishers, services providers, or directly by the author—embraces the spirit of entrepreneurship. It offers writers more sovereignty over their work. The road to publication is typically quicker, and the financial return per book sold may be higher. Yet, this path demands a significant personal investment, both in terms of time and money, and the challenge of standing out in a saturated market.

Expectations Vs. Reality

Many writers dream of being that unknown who gets a six-figure advance from a Big 5 publisher and becomes a *New York Times* best-selling author overnight. In this dream, the author also owns their copyright and receives high royalties and gives up their job to only write full time from exotic locales for their adoring fans. Oh, and they never have to market the book themselves. The author wakes content and hopeful.

Let's look at another dream, one of becoming a published author, but this time, the journey is quite different. In this dream, the writer crowdfunds their book and marketing efforts by creating future superfans who feel invested literally and figuratively in the author and their story. The author communicates regularly with their readers and keeps them up to date on the book's progress. Lots of hard work, communication, and marketing by the author leads to books that connect easily to the readers because of their hands-on involvement with every aspect of the process. The author wakes content and proud of their accomplishment.

Both are wonderful dreams, but the stark reality is that the likelihood of an unknown writer getting a Big 5 traditional deal is very slim. It's not impossible, but let's just say, the stars' alignment would be imperative to make this dream come true. However, the author who dreams of a hands-on journey, includes readers in the process, and crowd funds, has a very good chance of making their publishing dream come true. Both published authors—one hopeful and one in control.

The key in deciding how you publish your book is to do a lot of research and apply that knowledge to the goals you have for yourself and the book. Be objective when weighing the pros and cons of each publishing business model. Remember that *you* have the story; interview *them*. You are your best (and sometimes only) advocate.

TRADITIONAL PUBLISHING

In the quest to transform your manuscript into a printed book gracing the shelves of bookstores, traditional publishing stands as a beacon of aspiration for many authors. Grasping the terminology around this industry is a cornerstone, not just for communication, but for the successful navigation of the publishing landscape. Let's clarify aspects of traditional publishing and create a deeper understanding of this revered path to authorship.

The terms to be unpacked are many: literary agent, query letter, manuscript submission, acquisition editor, book advance, royalties, distribution channels, and book marketing. This also outlines the process your book will take when seeking a traditional deal.

A literary agent will serve as your gatekeeper. Make sure the agent you choose is familiar with your genre and has access to the publishers you are familiar with. You acquire an agent by crafting a captivating one-page pitch called a query letter conveying the essence and potential of your manuscript. Basically, your query letter acts as a job application for your book; make it stand out.

Upon securing an agent, the manuscript submission becomes your next milestone. This is the full draft of your book, polished to near-perfection, ready for the agent to present to publishers. Here, the acquisition editor enters the scene. For intents and purposes, they act as the talent scout, constantly seeking the next big thing. They assess your work's marketability, its fit within their catalog, and its potential to captivate readers. The acquisition editor will also consider your author platform and following.

Once the book is picked up and the deal is inked, you may receive a small advance against future royalties. In a nutshell, you may get $5k at signing, but until the publisher makes back all they invest in your books with marketing, PR, editing, design, etc., the likelihood of seeing any royalties is slim. Royalties also, if earned, will be smaller than Hybrid, Service Providers, or Self-Publishing.

Here is an important sidenote regarding the publishing agreement, always make sure you own your copyright! Along with this, hire an experienced lawyer to go over the legalese of the document.

The biggest plus for traditional publishing aside from the prestige is distribution. Distribution channels with traditional publishers will get you in all the bookstores the sales force can manage, as well as libraries and online retail throughout the world.

Once the book is out, not unlike any other form of publishing, the authors will take part in marketing efforts. Though the author does not pay for this upfront, they will be required to "work the room" and be available when the publisher needs them to promote the book.

The potential rewards are substantial: a professionally edited and designed book, a structured marketing plan, and the street cred that comes with being a traditionally published author.

In conclusion, traditional publishing is a complex and competitive field that demands not only a compelling manuscript but also a thorough understanding of its key terms.

HYBRID PUBLISHING

Hybrid publishing functions as a midway point between DIY and traditional publishing. Publishers in the hybrid model vet submissions and rarely need an agent to submit them. Authors invest monetarily in their book's production and partner with the experienced hybrid to benefit from professional editing and design, as well as distribution channels and marketing acumen. Royalties in hybrid publishing are usually higher than in traditional deals, reflecting the author's financial contribution and partnership.

Publishing agreements vary from one to three years, including distribution of all formats (eBook, paperback, or hardcover). Authors retain ownership of their copyright.

Distribution channels in hybrid publishing vary, but as the Independent Book Publisher's Hybrid Criteria states, Amazon cannot be the only distribution option. A robust network is vital for a book's success, and hybrid publishers often have established connections and resources which authors may lack.

Hybrid publishers may vary in marketing author's books. Some hybrids partner with authors in creating a marketing strategy and implementation, while others provide no marketing options. Marketing efforts are rarely included in the publishing package pricing, requiring additional fees.

Hybrid publishing is not just a model—it's a manifesto for the modern author, a declaration of independence with an acknowledgment of the power of partnership. It represents a shift in the publishing paradigm, offering a bespoke journey for each unique narrative, ensuring your story finds its target reader. Hybrid publishing combines the best of parts of traditional and self-publishing. (And yes, I'm a little biased on this one . . . insert wink here)

SELF-PUBLISHING

Many authors who either become disillusioned with agent responses and long wait times decide to self-publish or author publish. While this can be the alternative to investing in a hybrid publisher, there are pros and cons as well.

Let's first cover the elephant in the room when it comes to self-publishing: perception. Self-published authors must hold their books to the high standards of traditional and hybrid publishers. It must look professional to be accepted by your reader.

The prerequisites for self-publishing are straightforward yet vital. You will need a polished, edited manuscript, a captivating cover design, a formatted interior, an understanding of various publishing platforms, and a plan for marketing and distribution. Consider a budget for potential expenses, such as professional editing, design, and marketing.

Engage a professional editor to refine sentence structure, grammar, and narrative coherence of your manuscript. A fresh pair of eyes will often catch what you might overlook. Though an editor is a tangible cost, it will take your manuscript to the next level and ensure your story perception is as professional as possible.

They say you can't judge a book by its cover, but the truth is, that saying was never about books. The cover is your book's first impression. It's a three-second chance to create interest. Invest in a professional cover designer whose style resonates with the genre and your story.

Interior formatting is your next challenge. The text must not only be legible but also aesthetically pleasing. Whether you hire a professional or tackle this task yourself, ensure consistency in font choice, margins, and spacing and adhere to book publishing standards.

With design elements in place, select your publishing platform. Kindle Direct Publishing offers direct access to Amazon and a vast readership, while IngramSpark will allow you to access the most distribution channels with one upload.

Also, keep in mind all marketing efforts will also be on your shoulders as well.

I will add that an alternative to self-publishing but without quite the hybrid financial commitment is to hire a service provider publisher who will, for a fee, help you through the publishing process. You pay for services you need upfront. The book release concludes the service provider's obligations unless you need more services at additional fees. This may be an excellent compromise for those with smaller budgets.

In the end, remember that publishing is a journey, not a race. Savor the process, learn from the waves, and allow yourself to grow as both a writer.

TRADITIONAL PUBLISHING (the Big 5 and some independent presses)

Pros

- **Prestige and Validation:** Traditional publishers have the reputation of being the pinnacle of publishing.
- **Professional Editing and Design:** Publishers provide layout, cover design, and professional editing services.
- **Marketing:** To help you promote your book, traditional publishers have distribution and sales networks along with marketing and publicity departments.
- **Distribution & Sales:** Traditional publishers will have a sales team and established distribution channels into stores, both online and brick & mortar and libraries.

Cons

- **Strictly Competitive:** Traditional publishing is extremely selective of agent submissions, with few spaces available for publication.
- **Agent:** You will have to find an agent that pitches your genre to the publisher.
- **Loss of Creative Control:** Publishers have the last word on cover design and editorial adjustments, unless specifically negotiated in the contract.
- **Lengthier Process:** The traditional publishing process takes considerably longer because of the addition of finding a literary agent to pitch your work. Once you have an agent, it is up to them to submit your work to traditional publishers. This sometimes involves several rounds of submissions,

discussions, and more edits. Once accepted by the publisher, the process can take eighteen months to two years based on their release schedule.

- **Lower royalty:** While some traditional publishers may give a small advance, many authors see no royalties, since the publisher must recoup their investment before paying additional author royalty.

The Big 5 Publishers are: Penguin/Random House, Hachette, Simon & Schuster, Harper Collins, and Macmillan

HYBRID PUBLISHING

Pros

- **Achieving a Balance of Control and Support:** Hybrid publishing provides experts to create a professional book and partnership in publishing and marketing.
- **Access to Distribution Networks:** Hybrid publishers have distribution networks of varying types to ensure your book will go to its intended market.
- **Vetted Submissions:** Hybrid publishers provide professional editing and design to the works they accept at their discretion to publish. Not all submissions are accepted.
- **Higher royalties:** With a paid hybrid partnership, authors see quicker royalty disbursement and usually higher royalty pay outs.
- **Detailed contract agreements:** Hybrid publishers will have an agreement (contract) outlining their partnership with the author for a certain length of time. It also will detail the royalty split and how payments are paid. Other details included such as author copyright ownership and author vs publisher responsibilities.

Cons

- **Cost Factors:** Hybrid publishing is a paid partnership, with pricing ranges based on the services offered.
- **Track Record:** Do your homework before choosing a hybrid publisher to make sure they have a solid track record and support your publication objectives and goals.
- **Varying Quality:** Many Service Providers call themselves Hybrid Publishers but do not provide the support, not the high-quality criteria of a hybrid. Ask if you can interview some of their current authors. Examine their websites thoroughly and flag questionable offerings.

SERVICE PROVIDER PUBLISHERS

Pros

- **No submission or vetting process:** Service Provider Publishers will publish most works submitted.
- **Access to Editors, Designers, and Marketing:** Service Provider Publishers offer professionals for each service you will need.
- **Flexible Packages:** Service Provider Publishers provide a range of service packages.
- **Higher royalties:** With this type of publisher, authors may see higher royalties than hybrid or traditional deals because they are hands off after publication.

Cons

- **Cost Factors:** Service provider publishers require payment upfront before publishing.

- **Quality:** Make sure you read reviews and fine print as to the process of publishing. Ask questions about the professionals who will edit and design your book. Ask for samples.
- **Distribution and availability:** Many service providers have limited distribution using only KDP.

SELF-PUBLISHING (AUTHOR PUBLISHING)

Pros

- **Total Creative Control:** If you author-publish your book, you have complete creative control over every element of your book, including the content, the cover, and the price.
- **Shorter Time to Market:** Bypassing the drawn-out process of submissions, self-publishing enables you to publish your book whenever you choose.
- **100% Royalties:** Authors who self-publish often receive the highest percentage of royalties.

Cons

- **Self-Promotion:** Every aspect of promoting your book will be your responsibility, whether you do it yourself or you hire marketing help.
- **Initial Investment:** Professional editing, cover design, and marketing services are upfront fees.
- **Perception Issues:** Despite self-publishing's increasing popularity, some readers and industry insiders still harbor prejudices toward this model.
- **Investment:** While it is up to the author how much they do themselves and how much they choose to spend on professional help, the investment may

become greater than with hybrids or service providers because of the author's lack of knowledge
about the publishing industry.

WRITE A DESCRIPTION OF YOUR BOOK

You're going to need an excellent description of your
book; both for the back of your book and for marketing. It can be very easy to go overboard with this, limit
it to 300 words at the most. Keep in mind this is marketing text, rather than the writing you've done in your
book. Putting that another way, it's copywriting, rather
than book writing. You should study other books in your
genre or comp titles to see how certain phrases and pacing should read.

If you are uncomfortable writing in this manner,
you may want some professional help. This description
should be something that publishers and marketers can
use, as is, without having to rewrite it. Regardless of
whether you write the description of your book or have
someone else do it, you want to make sure that you go
back to your beta readers and have them look at it, too.
Ask them whether that description would make them
want to read the book. That's really all that matters.

The synopsis is your first chance to excite your
reader about your story. While the cover may get them
intrigued, the copy will inspire them to "buy now."

WRITING EXERCISE 1

Spend some time reading the synopsis and back cover
copy of books in your genre. Get a feel for what readers

are looking for. Now write yours. Get feedback from your beta readers on this copy as well.

WRITING EXERCISE 2

For this exercise, go back to your story why—why you wrote the book. The book is complete, and you have a better idea which publishing model would be the best fit. Be sure to weigh in your core goals and why you wrote it.

On top of four pages, write each of these publishing models: Traditional, Hybrid, Service Provider, and Self-Publishing. Divide these pages into Pros and Cons, and you will fill-in the columns based on your personal goals.

When you have made your list and decision, research publishers in that category or categories. Look for reviews from other writers, contact current authors, find out if they publish your genre and are looking for submissions. Will you need an agent? Will you need to crowdfund? Think about every aspect of the process, from financial to time, to creative control, when making your choice.

Pro tip: With every model except self-publishing, make sure there is a contract or agreement that is acceptable and fitting with your goals. Make sure you will own your copyright and be aware of the duration of your contract. It may be beneficial to have a lawyer's help.

CONCLUSION

"If you're walking down the right path and you're willing to keep walking, eventually you'll make progress."–Barack Obama

I f you have made it this far, we've gone on an exciting journey together. Taking the story you've always wanted to tell, turning it into an actual book that is not only intriguing but written with your reader in mind, is an accomplishment you should be proud of. You are on the way to being a published author with a book that your reader won't be able to put down.

This process may seem long and sometimes tedious, but every part is necessary to stay focused. While there is no one source I can point to, where a successful writer has detailed these steps as the ones they have taken, there are many successful writers who have talked about various parts of this process. What I've done is assemble everything into an actionable plan; something that you can use to make your own book planning process a success. These are real-world methods you will not find in a classroom.

Keep your eyes open for additions to our "Words Matters" series, as we dive deeper into storytelling, cover design, editing, marketing, and more. I want to ensure your successful writing career by sharing what I've learned so you can avoid mistakes I've made.

One last thing, I'd like to ask you for one favor. You will quickly learn this will be a big ask that you, too, will incorporate in your final note to your readers: *please give me a positive review on Amazon.com.* Positive reviews help sell a book above anything else. I thank you in advance.

I wish you the best of luck on your story's journey. Enjoy the ride.

In gratitude,

Julee

AUTHOR BIO

For over thirty years, JuLee Brand's experience includes being an award-winning graphic designer and over ten years of publishing experience working as an Art Director at Hachette Books Nashville and founding the award-winning W. Brand Publishing, a hybrid boutique publisher specializing in memoirs and fiction where she is the acting publisher and art director/designer.

Her career includes over eighteen years as a television graphics designer/animator at High Five Entertainment, and several years teaching graphic design as an adjunct professor at Belmont University in Nashville, Tennessee. Since 2000, Brand's design firm, designchik, has specialized in branding/identity/marketing for small businesses and serving the music, book, and television industries.

In her spare time, she is an aspiring author, wine connoisseur, wanderlust traveler, and mom to a floof named Henry. She lives in gratitude every day.

Made in the USA
Las Vegas, NV
05 March 2024

86725614R00066